COURAGEOUS

Also by Michael Healey:
Kicked
The Drawer Boy
Plan B
Rune Arlidge
The Innocent Eye Test
Generous

with Kate Lynch:
The Road to Hell

COURAGEOUS
MICHAEL HEALEY

PLAYWRIGHTS CANADA PRESS
TORONTO

PLAYWRIGHTS CANADA PRESS
The Canadian Drama Publisher
215 Spadina Ave., Suite 230, Toronto, ON Canada M5T 2C7
phone 416.703.0013 fax 416.408.3402
orders@playwrightscanada.com • www.playwrightscanada.com

For professional or amateur production rights, please contact
Pam Winter, Gary Goddard Agency
10 St. Mary Street, #305
Toronto, ON
M4Y1P9
phone 416-928-0299, email pamwintergga@bellnet.ca

The publisher acknowledges the support of the Canadian taxpayers through the Government of Canada Book Publishing Industry Development Program, the Canada Council for the Arts, the Ontario Arts Council, and the Ontario Media Development Corporation.

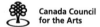 Canada Council for the Arts   Conseil des Arts du Canada    ONTARIO ARTS COUNCIL CONSEIL DES ARTS DE L'ONTARIO

 Canada   Ontario
Ontario Media Development Corporation

Cover image by Alessandro Paiva
Cover and type design by Blake Sproule

LIBRARY AND ARCHIVES CANADA CATALOGUING IN PUBLICATION

Healey, Michael, 1963-
Courageous / Michael Healey.

A play.
ISBN 978-0-88754-930-4

I. Title.

PS8565.E14C68 2010   C812'.54   C2010-904064-3

First edition: August 2010
Printed and bound in Canada by Canadian Printco, Scarborough

Courageous premiered at the Tarragon Theatre, Toronto, on January 6, 2010, with the following cast and crew:

Tom Barnett	Tom
Patrick Galligan	Brian Till
Erin MacKinnon	Tammy
Melissa MacPherson	Lisa
Brandon McGibbon	Todd Going
Tom Rooney	Martin Guest/Pete
Maurice Dean Wint	Arthur Aboulela/George Ambali

Director	Richard Rose
Stage manager	Kinnon Elliot
Set and costume design	David Boechler
Lighting design	Andrea Lundy
Sound design	Todd Charlton

The play subsequently opened at the Citadel Theatre, Edmonton, on February 25, 2010, with the following cast changes:

Patrick McManus	Tom
Ari Cohen	Brian Till
Michael Healey	Martin Guest/Pete

Courageous was developed during a residency at the Banff Centre and also in workshop readings at the Shaw Festival and Tarragon Theatre. My thanks to Richard Rose, who provided excellent insight at critical moments. He then assembled a matchless premiere production.

CHARACTERS

Tom
Tammy
Brian Till
Lisa
Todd Going
Martin Guest
Pete
Arthur Aboulela
George Ambali

ACT ONE SCENE ONE

The house light goes down and the following is projected somewhere:

> Although much of our life is rooted in the anxiety of time, in other words the fear of death, the continuity of knowledge and wisdom that has brought us here together is rooted in love, a love that is not only as strong as death, but able to cast out its fear.
>
> —Northrop Frye

The above fades and is replaced by the following:

> The trouble with equality is that no one actually wants to be treated just like everybody else.
> —Michael Ignatieff

An office on the third floor of New City Hall in Toronto: small, curved, wood-panelled, with no apparent windows. A desk. A half-dozen chairs for witnesses.

Lights come up to find TAMMY, *twenty, in the middle of the room. She's wearing a dress and heavy boots. She holds a bouquet containing three sunflowers. Her boyfriend,* TODD, *has on a jacket, shorts, and holds a tie in one hand.* TAMMY's *best friend,* LISA, *is wearing a low-cut top and holds a small camera.* TAMMY *is screaming.*

Also in the room are TOM, *thirty-eight, sitting at the desk, and* ARTHUR, *late twenties.* ARTHUR *is Sudanese. He sits quietly in a corner chair.*

TAMMY   I DON'T CARE! HOW CAN YOU TELL ME THAT?

LISA   Because it's true.

TAMMY   I DON'T CARE!

LISA   Well, you should.

TAMMY   No I shouldn't. I don't have to. I don't have to care, because even if it's true, you're only telling me because of something you want, because you want something, not because you're my friend. You're supposed to be my friend.

LISA   I am your friend.

TAMMY   No you're not! A friend wouldn't say that like that. A friend would like, be a friend. You have your own thing here, and because of that, what you say is invalid! Even if it's true. You want something here, I know you do, you always did. From like the first day I ever came to you and said, like, "What do you think of Todd Going," and you were like: "He's okay, I don't know, a bit of a dork but nice, I don't know," and I went: "Because I totally want him," ever since then you've been out to wreck it. So I don't care. I don't care if you like did whatever you did. If you like blew him, okay? I don't fuckin' care.

TOM   If I may—

TAMMY   Because if you blew him, or whatever you did, it wasn't from love, and I know that. It was from like the opposite of love. Because he and I are in love, and so your thing, the thing you did, was just from hate, your hate, and his, like, being a stupid guy. *(wheeling on* TODD*)* Right? Right?

TODD   Uh, yes.

TAMMY   That's right. He's a stupid guy, and he knows it. Or, like, he's a guy, and what guy in the history of the world has ever said no to getting blown.

TOM   You know, Tamara, I think that this—

TAMMY   So he's out of this, okay? This is just your shit. Yours and my shit.

TOM   —should be resolved, perhaps, not here, but—

LISA   I don't have any shit. You have shit. Like being blind to what kind of a guy your boyfriend is, like that kind of shit.

TAMMY   No, no, no. I know he's an asshole. I know it. That's the thing in this you never got. I know it. Look at him. Who wears shorts to get married?

TODD   Yeah, these were the only things that were clean this morn—

TAMMY   But we are in love, okay? We are in love, okay? That's empirical. That's the empirical knowledge part of this. That's the thing nobody ever got.

LISA   That's the thing. You're not. You're not in love—

TAMMY   YES WE ARE. And you can't stand that. So just admit that you can't stand that, admit that's why you blew Todd, and then just stand there AND BE MY FRIGGIN', LIKE, MAID OF HONOUR!

    A pause.

LISA   Yeah. Okay.

TAMMY   Good. *Fuck. (to* TOM*)* Okay. Sorry. We're all set.

        A beat.

TOM   All right then. Tammy, you stand over here, just here, that's
        right, and then Lisa, you can be just here, okay, or, okay,
        wherever you like, and Todd—

TODD   Can you, hey, sir, do you know how to do one of these?

        TODD *means his tie.* TOM *looks down at the tie he's currently
        wearing. He holds it up for* TODD *and smiles.*

        Oh! I guess you can! For sure! Okay, can you do mine?

TOM   Of course.

        TOM *takes* TODD*'s tie, begins to tie it by placing it around his
        own neck.* TODD *wants to speak, decides against it, waits.*
        TOM *finishes the tie, loosens it, and hands it over to* TODD*.*

TODD   Oh, good. I kind of thought you were going to wear it.

TAMMY   He was just doing it up, baby.

TODD   I know, it's just that he did it around his own, like, so I was
        like, "What the fu—"

TAMMY   I know, sweetie. Okay. Okay?

TOM   Okay. Just here, and, that's right. *(to* LISA*)* Just no pictures
        during the actual ceremony, all right? As many as you want
        after.

LISA   Sure, whatever.

TOM   Good. Now Tamara, Lisa will be your witness, right? And
        Todd, did you have someone to be your witness today?

TODD   Oh. Oh, like, crap.

TAMMY   OH JESUS!

TODD   No, I forgot to tell you, he like called, last night? And—

TAMMY   JESUS CHRIST!

TODD   My mom took the message. But, so—

TOM   That's all right, Todd.

TAMMY   No it's not! We need a witness. On the website, it said two witnesses, and YOU KNEW THAT!

TODD   No, I did know that, but Mom took the message from Jord, and she never gave it to me, because we were like, you know, in my room and whatnot.

TOM   It's okay.

TODD   We were, you know, starting the honeymoon early. You know? Which was your idea, starting the honeymoon early.

TOM   It's okay.

TODD   *(to TOM)* We were doing it.

TOM   Yes.

TAMMY   We need two witnesses!

LISA   Maybe you should do it another day. Come back.

TAMMY   OH YEAH, YOU'D LIKE THAT, BITCH—

TOM   OKAY! Okay. So, we can work around the witness problem, it's no problem, really, we can—

TODD   What about that dude? Can we use him?

TODD means ARTHUR.

Can we use you, sir?

A beat. ARTHUR rises.

ARTHUR Of course.

ARTHUR crosses to the group.

I am Arthur Aboulela.

TODD Awesome. That's great. I'm Todd? Todd Going?

ARTHUR looks TODD in the eye, warmly shakes TODD's hand.

ARTHUR It is an honour to participate.

ARTHUR takes TAMMY's hand.

Hello.

TAMMY Hello.

TAMMY, held in ARTHUR's gaze, softens.

Hello. Thank you.

ARTHUR Thank *you*. I am pleased to be here. This will be a day you shall never forget.

TAMMY Yes. I… I hope so.

ARTHUR Oh, yes. And you! What is your name?

LISA Lisa.

ARTHUR Lisa. We have an important job, have we not? We are to be their, their, spines for them! At this occasion. It is a great honour to do this for a loved one, yes?

ARTHUR is so warm that LISA is forced to smile. She even becomes a little shy.

LISA   Yes.

ARTHUR   Yes. It is a great thing you are all doing. To be free people, to make choices for yourselves, these are great things, are they not? These are things we must never take lightly. Not everyone in the world has this freedom, do they? Now. Where must I stand?

TOM   Just here.

ARTHUR   Yes.

They arrange themselves before TOM. The lights fade. Blackout.

ACT ONE SCENE TWO

In the black, the flash of a camera goes off. As the lights come up, TOM is taking photos of the wedding party. ARTHUR is improbably tall in this group.

TOM   Now the women.

TAMMY and LISA look at each other warily.

LISA   Aw, c'mere, you dumb twat.

TAMMY   I love you too.

TAMMY, relieved and soppy, throws herself into LISA's arms. TOM takes the photo.

TOM   Now the men.

ARTHUR and TODD pose. ARTHUR grasps TODD's hand and holds it over his head like a prizefighter.

TODD   All right! Woooo!

ARTHUR Yes! Wooo!

> *The photo session ends. Hugs all around.* ARTHUR *gives* LISA *a card.*

I would be very grateful if you could send me a copy of these photos. This is my email address.

LISA   Yes, I will.

ARTHUR Yes. I know you are a good friend to her.

> LISA *hugs* ARTHUR.

TODD   *(to* TOM*)* So, thanks for everything.

TAMMY   Yes, thank you.

TOM   It's my pleasure. The documents will be sent to your house.

TODD   Oh, but...

TOM   Yes?

TODD   I thought we were married now.

TOM   That's right.

TODD   No, but I mean, like right now.

> *A beat.*

TOM   You are.

TODD   So, but, like we don't have to wait for like the mail to show up? Because sometimes the mail doesn't get to our house, and sometimes my sister takes it and smears—

TOM   No, the papers don't matter. You're married now. You're all done.

TODD   I'm all done. Okay! We're all done!

> *TODD sweeps TAMMY off her feet and the wedding party leaves. TOM notices LISA's camera, left behind on a chair. TOM picks it up and starts after them.*

TOM   Hey! Guys! You forgot your...

> *He exits. A beat of ARTHUR alone. TOM returns after a moment, empty-handed, and gives ARTHUR an amused, harried look.*

Wow.

> *ARTHUR smiles.*

I'll just write this up, and then we can go.

> *TOM goes to the desk and ARTHUR returns to his chair. A long, quiet moment of TOM assembling papers, writing. ARTHUR is quite still. TOM looks up and ARTHUR meets his gaze. They smile at each other. Then TOM resumes his work. Silence. After some time there is a knock at the office door and BRIAN Till sticks his head in.*

BRIAN Hi. Sorry. Is this the marriage office?

TOM   Yes. Come in.

> *BRIAN enters with MARTIN Guest. They are close in age, though it's possible MARTIN is a little older. They wear dark suits with matching ties.*

BRIAN Hi. The name is Till. I've got a marriage appointment today. I mean—

TOM   Oh.

TOM finds a file, checks something.

Yes. Till and... Guest?

MARTIN Martin Guest, yes, that's me.

TOM That's funny. The way it's written here, Till and Guest, because "guest" is in lower case for some reason, it looks like you didn't know who you'd be marrying, so they just wrote "and guest."

A beat.

Sorry.

MARTIN We're early.

BRIAN Yes. We were supposed to be here for one o'clock. But I was wondering if we could push it up?

MARTIN He has a lunch.

BRIAN Don't say it like that.

MARTIN What. What did I say? You have a lunch.

BRIAN Okay. *(to TOM)* I have a lunch with a client, it's unavoidable, and God knows I'm going to pay for it at home, but my question, my question to you is, can you marry us now instead of at one?

TOM My colleague Rebecca is scheduled to perform your service. She's not here right now. I expect her quite soon.

BRIAN I see. Is there any way, I mean, can you perform our marriage?

TOM You're Rebecca's service.

BRIAN Yes. And, because of my scheduling conflict, I wonder if we can become your service?

TOM Yes, let me...

TOM, quite calmly, consults several files and schedules. MARTIN and BRIAN look at each other, MARTIN looks away. He notices ARTHUR.

MARTIN Hello.

ARTHUR Hello.

MARTIN looks at ARTHUR, trying to place him. ARTHUR smiles.

TOM No, I'm sorry. But Rebecca will be here in about a half an hour.

BRIAN I see.

A pause.

MARTIN Do you want to make a phone call?

BRIAN Do I want to make what phone call? To who?

MARTIN Do you want to make the "I can't make it to the lunch, I'm getting married" phone call?

BRIAN Martin...

MARTIN Think very carefully before you answer that question, okay, Brian?

A pause.

BRIAN I—

MARTIN Look, okay, I know who I am in this. I know that I have no standing here, that you're who you are and I'm just who I am, that you have the important job and I work in a... where I work, that you get to make all the decisions and that I get to live with them, okay? I get who I am in this. And I understand that underlying everything here, since the day we met, is that I in some unspoken way should be grateful to even be in this relationship. And Brian, look at me: I am. I am. But my self-esteem is taking a beating here, and my desire to be with you is going to catch some of that beating really, really soon.

A pause. BRIAN *takes out his phone.* MARTIN *has turned to* ARTHUR.

Sorry. Hello. Have we met?

ARTHUR We have.

There is something in ARTHUR's *response that makes* MARTIN *decide not to pursue the question.* MARTIN *turns to* BRIAN, *who can't make the call.*

BRIAN *(to* TOM*)* Hi, sorry, is there any way that you can squeeze us in? Or that you can accommodate us?

TOM I'm sorry.

BRIAN Could you, I don't know, start the process, the ceremony, and then your colleague could take over when she gets here. Or something?

TOM I'm afraid not. There can only be one officiant. For the records.

BRIAN Yes, I understand the horror that might occur from a breach in the bureaucratic order here, but I wonder if you could friggin' help us out.

A beat. TOM *is pleasant.*

TOM I'm sorry.

BRIAN You, look, you perform these things, right? You have that power?

TOM I have.

BRIAN So I don't see, I mean, the office is empty, we are next up on the list, yes, we're early, but still, we are next, you're here, we're here, I just, I don't know why you can't be a decent person and help us out. It's just decency, is all I'm asking for.

MARTIN Brian.

BRIAN No, I mean, sometimes, I understand, in certain jobs, government jobs, the mentality becomes, it becomes narrow. Stick to procedures. Do what is expected, no more, no less. Put in your time. Eight hours a day.

TOM Seven and a half, actually.

BRIAN Right. But you know out there, in the real world, people do jobs that aren't done until they're done. That require a greater commitment than just your time. That ask for risk, and your time, and, and the ability to think outside the narrow rules of your fucking job.

MARTIN I want to apologize for my future husband.

BRIAN No, don't do that. I just, I just want to know why you won't do your job.

        A pause.

TOM You don't have witnesses. You need two witnesses.

BRIAN It's a witness problem? If I find two witnesses, look there's one guy already, howareya, you okay being a witness today? Very happy event.

MARTIN Brian, he's probably not suitable.

BRIAN Sure he is, why not, what do you say?

MARTIN Brian, no.

BRIAN Why not? You got something against—

MARTIN This guy is the guy.

15

BRIAN   What guy.

MARTIN   The guy. From the bar.

BRIAN   What guy from the—

>*A beat.*

>This is the guy? From last, like, July?

MARTIN   Yes.

BRIAN   What's he doing here?

MARTIN   I don't know.

ARTHUR   I am waiting for my friend.

>*A beat.* BRIAN *turns to* TOM.

BRIAN   Is there anything that excludes a person that my boyfriend picked up one night because he was mad at me but too much of a pussy to say so from being a witness?

TOM   No.

BRIAN   And is there some reason why you couldn't act as our other witness?

TOM   Theoretically, no.

BRIAN   So? What's the problem?

>*A pause.* TOM *crosses the floor and* ARTHUR *stands.* TOM *kisses* ARTHUR.

TOM   Well, I always knew it was just a matter of time.

ARTHUR   Okay. You will be okay.

TOM turns to BRIAN and MARTIN.

TOM   I'm very sorry. I can't perform your wedding because the tenets of my faith don't allow me to marry homosexuals.

BRIAN   Your faith?

TOM   That's right. If you can just be patient and wait for Rebecca, she will be able to—

BRIAN   What does your faith have to do with it?

TOM   Rebecca will—

BRIAN   This is about us.

TOM   If you had come at the appointed hour—

BRIAN   This is, you know what? This is, you can't do this. You can't deny us the, the—

TOM   No one is denying you the—

BRIAN   I'm a lawyer, mister. Okay? I won't be pushed around like this.

TOM   It's not my intention to—

BRIAN   You can't do this!

MARTIN   Brian! It's okay. We'll wait.

BRIAN   The fuck we'll wait! The fuck we will!

Blackout.

ACT ONE SCENE THREE

A small, windowless meeting room at the Ontario Human Rights Commission, dominated by a table and several chairs. Apart from an Ontario coat of arms, there is no other decoration. The room is dimly lit, with pools of harsh light on the table. TOM is seated. His eyes are fixed. A long beat while TOM prays. The door opens and BRIAN enters. TOM crosses himself and rises.

TOM   Brian. Hello.

BRIAN is thrown by TOM's warmth.

BRIAN   Hello.

BRIAN and TOM shake hands. BRIAN waits to see where TOM will settle. He takes a chair some distance from TOM. There is a pause.

TOM   This shouldn't take too long, I guess.

A pause.

I thought your complaint was… eloquent, I suppose. Succinct. I enjoyed reading it.

A beat.

BRIAN   Thanks. Are you alone?

TOM   My partner said he was going to show up, but I haven't seen him.

BRIAN   No, I meant, do you have a lawyer?

TOM   I don't have representation. The archdiocese wanted to give me a lawyer, but I declined. They're very interested in this case, as you can imagine. But their goals here aren't the same as mine, so I declined the offer.

BRIAN   I see.

TOM   And you will represent yourself. I saw you on television last night.

BRIAN   Yes. They... they cut me off. I want you to know that. They used the worst, the harshest things I said, and threw out the rest.

TOM   I assumed as much. I hoped as much.

   A pause.

How is your partner, Mr. Guest?

BRIAN   I dunno. He's fine.

   A beat. BRIAN *goes to the light switch, turns up the lights. No longer dim, they are now just harsh.*

Do you mind?

TOM   Not at all.

BRIAN   This is, this is typical. Making us wait. The Ontario Human Rights Commission has a slightly condescending approach to the parties in a dispute. They always put the complainant and the respondent into a room before getting started, on the off chance they might work things out.

TOM   I see. It's nice. The system gives you every opportunity to work things out before the big shots get involved. I admire that. That optimism.

   A beat.

BRIAN   It's more that it's cheaper.

TOM   Of course.

        A pause.

        I want you to know, I harbour no ill will toward you for doing
        this.

BRIAN   Why not? Why don't you?

TOM   Well, I guess it's just not in my nature.

BRIAN   Your Christian nature.

TOM   Well, no, my personality. I gather there are plenty of people
        who share my faith who are more than willing to be antagonistic
        toward you. I'm just, I'm not one of them. And I also want you
        to know, I think you've got a reasonable complaint. And I'm
        sorry you were unable to get married the day you came to the
        office.

BRIAN   You are.

TOM   Yes, Brian, I am.

BRIAN   Sorry doesn't matter.

        A beat.

TOM   Well, no, I guess it doesn't matter to this proceeding.

        A pause.

BRIAN   You're Catholic?

TOM   Yes. Isn't that weird?

BRIAN   Well.

TOM   It is. I'll spare you the trouble of being polite. It is. Can I ask
        you something?

BRIAN   Sure.

TOM   When did you know you were gay?

       A beat while BRIAN *decides whether to answer.*

BRIAN   Third grade.

TOM   And did you choose it? Did you choose to be gay?

BRIAN   Of course not. It wasn't a choice. It was a... it was just a fact.

TOM   Yes. I was twelve. I was looking at somebody, it just... occurred to me.

BRIAN   Yes, that's... yes.

TOM   It wasn't long after that that I also realized I'd be a Catholic forever. It was just a fact, the same as being gay was a fact. I saw that I had a relationship with the Church that was much deeper, much more meaningful, than most people. I didn't will it, I didn't wish it, it just... there it was. But it wasn't long before I saw that these two facts were incompatible in so many ways.

BRIAN   How can you be part of a group that manifestly hates you?

TOM   Well, that's just people. The larger parts of the faith, its divine aspects, tend to dwarf whatever bullshit the people who call themselves my brethren can dish out.

       Also, one of the things I've come to understand is that part of your life is meant to be spent among people that wish you ill. It's part of the job of a Christian.

       A beat.

       So, as I say, it's nice to see you, Brian.

       BRIAN, *possibly against his will, laughs at this.* TOM *smiles.*

Can I tell you my feelings about gay marriage?

BRIAN   Maybe you should save that for the hear—

TOM   I don't understand why we want it so badly. It's so... as an institution, it's done more to oppress people, women mostly, than anything else I can think of. Why are we fighting to buy into that?

BRIAN   The only thing more oppressive than marriage is probably the Church.

TOM   Yes, very good, I'll give you that.

BRIAN   You will?

TOM   Of course. The Catholic Church is a nightmare in a lot of ways. Has been for a thousand years.

BRIAN   You're a... I guess you'd describe yourself as a progressive Catholic, then?

TOM   I'm not sure. But I would say that I've had to question every aspect of my faith in order to reconcile the gay me with the Catholic me.

BRIAN   I bet.

TOM   Yes. Imagine the contortions. Fortunately, there's usually a pretty clear line between the things that have to do with faith and the often ridiculous politics of my church. I mean, there's a huge difference between being a Catholic and being a Christian. The rules for being a Catholic are just... well, let's just say they're extensive. I've accepted some, the vast majority of them, and I actively question others. But the rules for being a Christian are much simpler. You could write them on a cocktail napkin. Don't kill each other, help each other out, that kind of thing. There are dozens of little opportunities in a day to practise being a Christian. Thirsty?

BRIAN   Sorry?

TOM   Can I get you some water?

BRIAN   No thanks.

TOM   Okay. *(a beat)* Anyway, marriage. Because I've never been a fan of the whole idea of it, I've never been able to join the fight for our right to it.

BRIAN   You're saying you don't believe in marriage at all? For anyone?

TOM   I think that for the vast majority of people it's more trouble than it's worth.

BRIAN   But marriage is what you, it's your job, for God's sake.

TOM   I love my job. I get to see people getting married, not being married. I'm there at the fun bit, and not for the horror to come. But also, Brian, and this might seem contradictory, as a Catholic, for me, marriage is a sacrament. And the sacraments aren't available to everyone, all the time. Taking holy orders is another sacrament, but I don't think I'll ever be someone who does that. There's a limited number of people who are qualified, for whom any given sacrament is available.

BRIAN   And I'm not qualified for this sacrament?

TOM   You're not, I'm afraid.

BRIAN   And why am I not qualified?

TOM   You mean apart from the fact that you're not a Catholic and the sacraments are meaningless to you?

BRIAN   Yes. What is it about me, personally, that disqualifies me from obtaining this thing?

TOM   Well, you're not going to like it.

BRIAN   I'm sure I won't.

TOM   It's because you'll never procreate.

> *BRIAN is about to object, TOM rushes on.*

Look, okay, look: the Catholic sacrament of marriage has two features: the union of two souls, which mirrors Christ's relationship with the Church, and the procreative, which mirrors man's mysterious relationship with God. That's what the sacrament is. That's it. It's one of the unarguable places my faith leads me to. It means that for us, it's something we simply don't have access to. But fortunately, you don't have to collect all seven sacraments to get into heaven. They aren't crucial, they're just, sort of, like bonus points. Deeply profound, very meaningful bonus points. And some people get some of them, and some people get others, and nobody gets all of them. Whatever else you want to say about it, the Catholic Church understands the concept of asymmetry. That sometimes, you don't get what everyone else gets.

BRIAN   But why shouldn't I get it? How is that not a form of discrimination?

TOM   Brian. You don't even want it. It doesn't mean anything to you. And here you are, prepared to get up on your hind legs to fight for your right to it.

BRIAN   It's the principle.

TOM   Principles only get us so far.

> *A pause.*

BRIAN   So, okay, you don't believe in marriage, and you also think that I don't deserve it.

TOM   Not at all. Of course you deserve to be married. It's just hard for me to be the one who marries you.

BRIAN   But you're performing civil marriages, not Catholic ones.

TOM   But I'm a Catholic who's doing it. And so I go to some lengths to make sure the marriages I can't reconcile with my faith go to someone else in the office.

BRIAN   But—

TOM   Look, you don't have to agree with my reasoning. I just want you to know that there *is* reasoning behind my behaviour. I just want you to know that I'm not some crazy self-loathing gay Catholic freak. I'm doing my best.

BRIAN   Whether you believe in it or not, marriage is our right. We have to protect every right that we've acquired.

TOM   I can't argue that. Although I hope that's not true in a few generations.

BRIAN   You don't think we'll have to defend our rights in the future?

TOM   Brian, I have a niece. She was raised by parents that were very active in securing women's rights—my brother and sister-in-law have fought so that their daughter can do whatever she wants in this society. And do you know what she does? My niece wears crop tops and low-rise jeans to school. She and her friends argue endlessly about makeup. Thanks to her parents, she gets to take questions of gender almost entirely for granted. That's my hope for our children.

I know I hurt you that day, deeply. Won't it be nice when all that happens is you're annoyed by a civil servant who's apparently too lazy to do his job?

BRIAN   But that's not the world we live in. In this world, there are rights, rules that society has chosen to live by, and when they are ignored, society loses meaning.

TOM   I don't disagree. But do you know what rights are? Rights are not rules. They represent wishes. We wish to have this kind of society, so we enshrine these prescriptions. We wish, for example, to have a tolerant society, so we give the individuals who are vulnerable certain protections. They're spelled out: for these people, these rights. But when we focus on the rule and forget the wish, then it's just institutionalized bullying. When you press your right to force me to marry you, it's not in the name of tolerance, because a tolerant person would find some way to respect my beliefs.

BRIAN   But at that moment, my rights trump yours. Clearly. My needs, what society has told me I can expect, my needs are more important than your right to your faith at that moment.

TOM   Which is the wrong way to look at the concept of rights. It's the common way to think of them, and it's the easiest way, but it's wrong. It's not about competition—my needs trump yours—rights are about humility.

It's human nature to bully one another. To use the power of the group to control individuals. But here—we're asked to do something massively difficult in this society. Here, the individual's liberty is supreme. And the only way to honour that ideal is to allow for the needs of others. We are required to set aside our human nature, to choose not to bully, and instead to make room for another. It's humility—choosing to defer to another when you don't have to—that defines the noblest part of our society. And it takes an enormous amount of courage to deny our instincts and defer to someone we could easily control. It's funny—it's a secular society we live in, but the thing we ask of ourselves is a Christian concept.

BRIAN   No, look, it's very simple: it's your job. You refused to do your job. And you work for the city, and I pay my taxes, and you shouldn't be in that job if your beliefs conflict with the job you agreed to do.

     A beat.

TOM   I want you to know I think you're right. That everything I say can be seen as just an excuse, because you're right. You have right on your side, Brian. The fact that I took the job before gay marriage was legal in this city is an excuse. The fact that our team is composed of four people, three of whom happily perform gay marriage, is an excuse. You're right, and you'll win at this tribunal, and you'll gain whatever compensation they feel is just, and I'll lose my job. But so what? What's the point of all of this?

BRIAN   It will right a wrong. I have a duty to do that, don't I? As a responsible citizen? I mean, what if it wasn't me that day? I mean, not a lawyer, not someone who knows the law, but just, two guys. Not bright guys, but in love, and they come in, and you tell them that they can't do what they've come to believe they have every right to do. And they don't have the intelligence to defend themselves, they don't know the law, and they leave, and their hearts break, and suddenly the promise society's made them is a lie. So they stop contributing to society and start just taking from it, or move to the States and take their high-paying jobs with them, or at the very least they come to understand that here, they are less than what they believed they were. If I can prevent that, because of my particular skill set, don't I have the moral obligation to do that?

          A beat.

TOM   I guess you do.

          A pause.

BRIAN   Look, maybe we can skip the formal part of the hearing, you seem, I mean, you seem to want to concede all the vital points. So maybe, for your comfort, so this isn't any worse than it has to be, we can ask them to skip to, to—

TOM   My judgment? Don't mistake my agreeableness for passivity, Brian. We'll have the hearing before the tribunal, every second of it. You're going to have to spell out exactly how you've been aggrieved, how I did it. What I did to you. Only by the relentless cataloguing of the harms I visited upon you can you make yourself available for the gift that's yours, if only you'll pause long enough to accept it.

BRIAN   What gift?

TOM   Forgiveness. You have the opportunity to forgive me.

A pause.

BRIAN   You said you'll lose your job?

TOM   Of course.

BRIAN   I thought you were already fired.

TOM   They announced my firing, which was widely reported. But my union intervened and I've been suspended, pending the outcome of this hearing. The press didn't report that because, I don't know, it wasn't as outrageous as me getting fired. But after your victory today, the city probably won't have much choice. Are we going to pretend I didn't just use the word "forgiveness"?

BRIAN   We are. I'm embarrassed by it. I don't know how to respond to it. It's the same as when you use words like "humility." I'm going to stick to the facts here and let the tribunal figure out how to resolve this.

TOM   Okay.

A pause.

BRIAN   No, you know what? Okay: that's exactly what people hate about you. About religious people.

TOM   What's that.

BRIAN   The constant blackmail. You look down on us, isn't that right? You might not put it that way, but you do. Anyone outside the faith is doomed, and therefore less than you. So you say "forgiveness," and if I don't choose it, whatever it means, then we both know you will forever have the moral high ground on me. You make me sound vulgar and heartless for choosing to defend myself. Well I'm sorry, but that's just manipulative.

TOM   But, Brian, I—

BRIAN   No. It's the way that people like you sidestep the law, responsibility, anything you don't want to deal with: "We believe something so profound it transcends your rules. You'll never understand, and you'll never be as right as us!"

TOM   It's not my faith you're mad at, it's me. It's how I come off. All my life, people have mistaken my low-key nature for some kind of spiritual conceitedness. Okay. Uh: LOOK, BITCH, WHO DO YOU THINK YOU ARE?

BRIAN   What are you—

TOM   No no, let's go, let's get it on. I don't want any moral high ground. Let's have it out, bitch. I REPEAT: WHO DO YOU THINK YOU ARE?

BRIAN   I'm, I'm a person defending my—

TOM   NO, BITCH, THAT'S WHAT YOU'RE DOING! Who you are is a man, a gay man, alive at the best time in history to be a gay man, IN THE BEST PLACE IN HISTORY TO BE A GAY MAN, and all you want to do is WRECK MY LIFE.

BRIAN   You tried to wreck my life when you—

TOM   LIKE FUCK I DID! I WAS JUST DOING MY JOB AND YOU ASKED FOR SPECIAL CONSIDERATION. YOU'RE THE LUCKIEST FUCKING ADULT IN HISTORY, AND STILL, WHEN YOU DON'T GET YOUR WAY, YOU DRAG SOMEONE TO THE ONTARIO MOTHERFUCKING HUMAN RIGHTS COMMISSION!

BRIAN   Could you—

TOM   I MEAN, FUCK! NO WONDER PEOPLE HATE US!

> *A beat.* TOM *giggles.*

I'm sorry, I just can't do that. I feel ridiculous. Sorry. Sorry I shouted.

BRIAN   It's... okay.

> *A pause.*

It's because people hate us. You must understand that, surely. It's *because* they hate us. There are people who will do whatever they can to take away our rights. That's why they have to be defended. I don't even, you know what? I don't even want to get married. But I will, mostly because Martin does. But I understand that act as something bigger than us. Because of where we are in history, because of this moment, because of how far we've come, our getting married is symbolically more loaded than any straight couple's marriage. For us, the event means so much that we'll never take it for granted. Every time we walk down the steps at city hall, it's like, I dunno, Mandela walking out of prison.

TOM   Yes.

BRIAN   It's a lot of pressure, actually, when you look at it like that.

TOM   Yes. Try not to.

BRIAN   Yeah.

> *A beat.*

TOM   You haven't done it yet? You haven't married Martin?

BRIAN   No. Not yet.

TOM   Our thing was months ago. There's no shortage of people who could have married you since then.

BRIAN   Yeah. I thought. Well. I thought that our getting married before this complaint of mine got resolved would weaken it.

TOM   Martin must be thrilled.

BRIAN   He's not happy. He...

TOM   He...?

BRIAN   No, nothing. We've been fighting. He didn't actually come home last night.

        TOM digests this.

TOM   I'm sorry.

BRIAN   Once this is resolved, we can go forward. It'll be fine. I mean, deep down, he understands. He knows what this means for, for the gay community. For all of us. Why I have to do it. He's not comfortable as a poster boy.

TOM   He just wants to be married.

BRIAN   Yeah.

TOM   Brian.

BRIAN   Yes?

TOM   Why are you asking for money from me. In this complaint.

BRIAN   Yes—

TOM   It's the only part of this I don't understand.

BRIAN   Yes. I know how it seems. But there are a limited number of ways I can request redress. I can't take from you your faith, which is the thing that got us into this whole mess. That would be a kind of direct compensation, and also has the benefit of insuring that no one else is subjected to this kind of discrimination. But your faith is yours. I have no right to it. I might have requested your getting fired or transferred out of your job. But I was under the impression that you'd already lost your job. So I wind up asking for money, mostly because I'm only allowed to ask for money. And I know how it sounds to say that. That I sound like a monster. But money's the only way… it's how we keep score, isn't it?

TOM   I don't have much money.

BRIAN   You have a condo. You have equity in that condo.

TOM   I… yes.

BRIAN   If they decide to award me what I've asked, you'll have to liquidate some of your assets.

>   *A beat.*

I have to treat you the exact same way I'd treat a redneck fag-hater who stopped us from walking into your office. You see that, don't you, Tom?

TOM   Yes I do.

BRIAN   There's a system in place, it's flawed maybe, it's imperfect, but it provides order. And order is how we get to call it society; order is all we have. The same order that lets you and me walk down a street holding our lover's hand is the thing that is being honoured here today. Do you see that, Tom?

TOM   But if—

BRIAN   No. Tom. Do you see that?

>   *A beat.*

TOM   I do.

BRIAN   The very words I wasn't allowed to say.

A pause. TOM *gets up.*

TOM   I can't... I suppose I can't believe I'm not angrier. Maybe there *is* something wrong with me.

Okay. Listen to me. All this will happen. You will win. It will not make you happy, or bring you any peace at all. It will make you worse, and it will probably poison your marriage, if you let it. If you do actually get married. I find I'm afraid for you, Brian. Not the way the pious are afraid for the souls of the unredeemed, not as a Catholic. I just don't see how this will do anything other than hurt you. I ask you for mercy, not for myself, but for your sake. I ask you once again to forgive me in your heart. Forgive me, Brian. Take my house, my job, ruin me in the press, do it all, but in your heart, forgive me my failing. If you don't, I'm telling you, this won't end well for you.

BRIAN   Is that a threat?

TOM   I—

BRIAN   That sounded like a threat. How else am I supposed to take that?

TOM   Brian.

BRIAN   *(rising)* I think I'll let them know we're ready to begin.

> BRIAN *walks past* TOM, *who grabs him. They struggle and* TOM *manages to embrace* BRIAN. *He holds him for several moments;* BRIAN *stops resisting. Suddenly* BRIAN *pushes* TOM *away, glares at him, and exits.*
>
> *Blackout.*

ACT ONE SCENE FOUR

A coffee shop. ARTHUR *sits in an alcove or banquette, a place that feels slightly enclosed. He sees someone enter and stands to wave.* MARTIN *comes to the table.* ARTHUR *sits;* MARTIN *remains standing.*

ARTHUR Won't you sit?

> MARTIN *hesitates, then sits.*

Your name is Martin.

MARTIN Yes. How did you get my cell—

ARTHUR It is not the name you gave me. When we first met.

MARTIN No.

ARTHUR You told me "Rodney." At that time.

MARTIN Yes. Well. I'm sorry.

ARTHUR I understand completely the impulse given the circumstance. I am Arthur Aboulela.

MARTIN Yes.

ARTHUR Would you like some coffee?

MARTIN All right.

ARTHUR Miss? Miss?

MARTIN I think you have to go to the counter to get what you want.

ARTHUR Nonsense. Miss? MISS?

A barista comes over. It's LISA from the first scene.

LISA   Is something wrong?

ARTHUR   Not at all. We would like—

LISA   Why are you shouting?

ARTHUR   We wish to have some coffee. I will have a Caffé Americano, and my friend here will have...

MARTIN   Uh, a latte. Extra foam.

LISA   You have to go up to the counter and ask me there.

ARTHUR   Nonsense. Here.

> *ARTHUR hands her a fifty.*

If there is any change, you may keep it. Thank you.

> *LISA looks at ARTHUR. He smiles. She leaves.*

It is my experience that the Canadian service employee is generally... reluctant to be helpful. They seem to need, remarkably, further incentive to do their job. Incentive beyond the fact that they are in a job.

MARTIN   Do you... understand our money?

ARTHUR   I feel I do.

MARTIN   It was a pretty big tip you gave her. That was a fifty-dollar bill.

> *ARTHUR sighs.*

ARTHUR   Was that gauche? I apologize. I hope she was not humiliated and that I did not embarrass you. I have been trained that the application of money is the only way to solve most problems, large ones and small ones. But since I have been here, I find that the offer of money is often the worst way of resolving things. Canadians tend to pretend they do not need it. To admit one needs money to get through one's day, even though this country is fantastically expensive, is apparently unthinkable. An interesting pretense.

MARTIN I don't think her feelings were hurt.

ARTHUR Let us hope not. All right. Martin. Can you guess why I have contacted you?

MARTIN I can guess.

ARTHUR Yes. Tomorrow your husband and my lover are to go before a human rights tribunal.

MARTIN Yes. My boyfriend. We aren't married yet. We're waiting until his complaint is resolved.

ARTHUR I see. Now, Martin. I am from Sudan. Do you know my country?

MARTIN I... a little. Not really. From the news.

ARTHUR Starving babies, men with machetes.

MARTIN Drought.

ARTHUR In fact the current problem is flooding, but yes. In my country, Martin, to go before a government body like the one they must face, it is very dangerous. I know it is not like that here, Tom is very calm about it; it is I who am afraid for him. I know it is not rational, but like handing over large denominations to get things done, it is something I cannot help. I fear for Tom. I ask you, Martin, do not let Mr. Till do this. Ask him to withdraw his complaint.

MARTIN I can't do that.

A beat.

ARTHUR I am resisting the temptation right now to offer *you* money.

MARTIN It won't do any good.

ARTHUR Are you sure? No amount?

MARTIN I'm saying I don't have that kind of influence with Brian. Even if I wanted to help you, even if I took your money, it wouldn't do any good.

ARTHUR He does not listen to what you say?

MARTIN Not often. He's very... he has a lot of scruples. He would call them.

ARTHUR Yes, he must do, because his behaviour seems irrational. The damage he will visit upon my Thomas is fantastically disproportionate to the slight he endured. Which is usually an indication that there are principles involved. Can you... do you think you could summarize his position?

MARTIN No. I don't think so.

A beat.

ARTHUR Is it safe to say that you do not share his conviction?

MARTIN I think his convictions are convenient. He's afraid of marriage. To me, at least. And this project has allowed him to delay the event.

ARTHUR It is very curious. The perception of Sudan is that people destroy each other casually and that the government turns a blind eye. And here we have a man who is willing to destroy another out of fear, because he is afraid to be married to you. And he will actually be aided in this by his government. Not that I wish to compare the genocide in my country to the rights-crazy culture of yours. I just mean: look how many ways people will find to hurt each other.

MARTIN Can I ask you a personal question?

ARTHUR Please do.

MARTIN Are you religious?

ARTHUR I was raised a Muslim. I no longer consider myself one. How could I be a conscientious Muslim and engage in the acts we have engaged in?

MARTIN But your lover, your Tom, is a Catholic?

ARTHUR Almost professionally so.

MARTIN The Catholic Church hates him. He's aware of that?

ARTHUR Of course he is. Is it not so brave of him? It is not possible to admire a man for his beliefs more than I do Tom.

A beat.

Of course, when you admire someone so very much, it sometimes makes it difficult to fuck him.

A beat.

I wonder if we have that in common, you and I. That we both have someone at home who is too busy shaping society to take care of the smaller things.

LISA arrives with the coffees.

Ah! Thank you so very much.

LISA Do you want sugar?

MARTIN No thanks.

ARTHUR   No thank you. Your name is Lisa, is it not?

LISA   Yeah, I thought I recognized you. How do I know you?

ARTHUR   You and I were witnesses at a wedding several months ago.

LISA   Oh fuck yeah!

ARTHUR   How is the happy couple doing?

LISA   I don't know. Pregnant. Good I guess. But what the fuck? Who gets married at twenty years old?

ARTHUR   Yes, your disapproval was palpable that day. And yet you agreed to be their witness. I think I admire that.

LISA   Yeah, well, she's my best friend. Even if she is stupid as fuck.

ARTHUR   *(to MARTIN)* She set aside her convictions to make someone happy. Is that not the noblest gesture a person can make?

MARTIN   Like I said, it's not me you have to convince. Brian is absolutely—

ARTHUR   Lisa, this is a man so inept in his thinking, he can't even tell when someone is coming on to him.

LISA   Really? *(to MARTIN)* You can't tell this guy's coming on to you?

MARTIN   I—

LISA   Fuck. Dude. I could see it from over there. Grab it while you can, Hondo, because you aren't getting any—

ARTHUR   *(rising and taking her hand)* It was nice to see you again, Lisa. All the best.

LISA   Yeah. All the best to you too. Good luck with that one.

         LISA goes. A pause.

MARTIN   What are you—

     LISA returns.

LISA   Hey, listen, did you mean for me to keep all that money?

ARTHUR   Absolutely, yes.

LISA   Wicked. Do you want like a scone or anything?

ARTHUR   *(to MARTIN)* Scone?

MARTIN   I... no.

ARTHUR   No thank you, Lisa.

LISA   Okay. Have a good night.

     She goes. There's a pause.

MARTIN   I'm trying to figure out if you believe that sleeping with me will somehow help the situation.

ARTHUR   I think you wildly overestimate my deviousness. Let me ask you: do you have an imagination?

MARTIN   I... yes.

ARTHUR   Yes. Can you imagine how boring it has been for me to live with someone who has decided to commit a kind of suicide? A person unwilling to forego his beliefs, choosing instead his own ruin, which consumes him to the point of being incapable of properly sucking my cock? He cannot focus, you see. Because he's sad. Or at prayer.

    It makes a person fantasize, does it not? And what do I, in my frustration, fantasize about? What seems dirtiest, and therefore the most fun? Having my cock properly sucked by the man engaged to the man who will be my lover's undoing.

And, Martin, while your imagination is engaged, think what this is like for someone like me. Do you realize how far I've come? I was born in a place where my survival depended on keeping a secret from myself, the secret of my sexuality. I had to deny the central fact of my being because of where I lived. And that is most of the world. It's something that you don't think of here—most of the world is not like this place. I think it a human trait, not just a Canadian one, to take for granted even the most incredible freedoms as quickly as they are won. But the world is mostly like I describe. Mostly, the world would kill us for contemplating the things we might do, the acts you and I have committed and will hopefully commit again. You, your country, is the exception; it is a majestic, safe, theme park of liberties, this place. And I made it here. Thanks exclusively to economics, incidentally. Thanks to my father's oil money. Certainly not through some Herculean act of will on my part.

And having got here, am I now to be denied my due amount of pleasure because my lover chooses to give up everything for a, a belief? A belief? He lives in a garden and he chooses to starve. Must I starve as well? I think not, Martin. How precious it seems, this dispute. It is precious. Like two children who would rather pull each other's hair instead of bend down and pick up an armful of candy, while others stand outside the fence of the park where they fight. When outside the fence, other human beings kill and kill for the simple reason that there's no better way to spend the time.

> *A beat.*

Martin, I won't have it. Will you join me? Does what I suggest hold any appeal for you?

> *MARTIN looks down.*

MARTIN Yes.

> *A beat.*

ARTHUR   Yes, it does. Because, I think, and you can tell me if this is not true, because this is a way of exerting some measure of control over your husband-in-waiting. It is not quite revenge, is it? It is borne from a need to be taken seriously by him, which is a need you feel almost constantly. It also, of course, has the tint of the self-destructive on it. And you have been having a little affair with that most of your life, yes?

MARTIN   That's right.

ARTHUR   Like many here. It has been my experience.

MARTIN   But that's not the only...

ARTHUR   Yes?

MARTIN   Also. I like you. I thought about you for a long time after we first met.

ARTHUR   Yes. People like me. It is amazing. This, in so many ways, is an amazing country. Who could know that simply by being forthright and free of self-loathing, that I would be enjoyed by so many here? Qualities which, I reiterate, would most certainly get me killed everywhere else, and here I am celebrated for them. Also, I find that people are charmed by my syntax. People assume I am good-natured and free of guile because of my speech. My capacity for wicked behaviour is constantly underestimated, primarily because I do not use contractions. Now. The question is where. Where shall we go to free me of my ridiculous situation, to punish your man, to celebrate our extreme good fortune?

     A pause.

MARTIN   I know a place.

ARTHUR   Good. Excellent. Shadowy, no doubt, slightly dirty. But slightly only.

     MARTIN smiles at ARTHUR.

ARTHUR rises. MARTIN gets up and they walk out together. As MARTIN passes ARTHUR, ARTHUR smacks MARTIN hard on the ass. They exit.

Blackout.

ACT ONE SCENE FIVE

TOM and ARTHUR's apartment. TOM sits, reading. The sound of a key in a door, and ARTHUR enters.

ARTHUR How was it? Is it over?

TOM They'll make a ruling in a few weeks' time. I expect he'll get whatever he asks for.

ARTHUR Because you didn't put up much of a fight?

TOM I certainly put up more of one than I thought I would. I think you would have been surprised. Had you been there.

     A beat.

Where were you last night?

ARTHUR I am leaving you. I will have to move out.

TOM You met someone?

ARTHUR I was with someone, yes. But I think it is best if we just regard him as leverage.

TOM I see.

ARTHUR Do you.

TOM I know I haven't been...

TOM sighs.

ARTHUR   Haven't been what?

TOM   I think you know exactly what I'm going to say.

ARTHUR   I believe I do, but I was hoping to hear some sort of apology before I left, so please continue.

TOM   You've been very supportive of me during a difficult time, and I've—

ARTHUR   I have been exactly as supportive as it's suited me to be. I suspect you could have used much more support. Start again. Apologize.

TOM   I know that at times it's felt like there are three in this relationship: you, me, and the Church. I know my faith makes you uncomfortable.

ARTHUR   My discomfort with your faith is nothing compared to the trouble it has given you. Apologize.

TOM   I'm not sure what you want me to say. What kind of apology you expect as you pack your bags and fuck off out the door. At the worst possible moment.

ARTHUR   I expect you to say: I led you here with a promise of something, and then failed to deliver on that promise. I want you to say: I lied. Do you know, it was two months I was with you before you told me you went to church four times a week, and not to the gym?

TOM   I told you I was a devout Catholic the night we met.

ARTHUR   Which I thought was just dirty talk.

A pause.

TOM   Please. I... I'm going through something horrible. And public. I'm not a strong person. Please. I need you.

ARTHUR   I think I must love you, because practically everything you say enrages me. Thomas. What is happening to you. You chose it, all of it.

TOM   I know, I know—

ARTHUR   Your faith has no real value in this society. Lip service is paid to the protection of religious freedom in this country, but in reality, people are mostly protected *from* religion. Do you know why? Because in every other place where religion is central, where it is valued by citizens, it abuses those citizens. Subjugates them. In the places where God is supreme, the people are not free.

TOM   My faith is a part of me. It gives my life meaning.

ARTHUR   I should give your life meaning.

TOM   Thank God you don't, since you're heading out the door. Thank God you don't, since you choose to fuck around on me all the time. Thank God you don't, since you've lied to me more times than I care to count.

ARTHUR   Catalogue the many ways I have abandoned you, big and small, over the last three years. Then ask yourself: where is God right now, at the worst moment of your life? I know it is not a fair comparison, me and God, because you entered into our relationship knowing that I would be intermittently promiscuous, but you went into your relationship with God knowing he would be *constantly* absent. It is the ultimate withholding, yes? And secretly, you believe His absence is all that you deserve.

TOM   Everyone thinks my relationship with God is just a symptom of some deep psychological problem. I'm constantly stunned that people refuse to take my faith seriously. People would rather believe I'm delusional than acknowledge that I'm engaged in something lifelong and profound. Fuck, no wonder I sneak to church.

ARTHUR You make yourself ridiculous when you—

TOM Arthur. I'm so scared. I love you. *Please don't leave me.*

A pause.

ARTHUR All right.

A beat.

TOM Thank you.

ARTHUR If you marry me.

TOM I... I can't...Why would you possibly want to—

ARTHUR My God! You understand nothing! You say you love me, you say you want me to stay, I ask for something simple, something which you say holds little meaning for you, and yet you hesitate when I ask for it! You thwart happiness at every turn! You fucking idiot!

TOM Why would you ask me to do something that you know is trouble for me? Something so loaded? It feels like a punishment. Is it? Is it a test? Why do you ask me for that?

ARTHUR I ask for it BECAUSE I WANT TO BE LOVED!

A beat.

I want love. And I want it from you, if possible. But if not from you...

A pause.

TOM Martin, Brian Till's boyfriend, he... he didn't come home last night either. Is it, were you...

ARTHUR Yes. And yes. I met him to plead your case. Which you can believe or not. In any event, he is my leverage. I am leaving you for Martin Guest. I have broken up your tormentor's nuptials, and I will now proceed to manipulate his ex-lover for as long as it suits me and then break his heart, and then move on to someone else. That is how much I love you. How much I did love you. Does that bring you no measure of comfort?

> *TOM says nothing. He's standing in a doorway that ARTHUR wants to get through.*

It's funny. It is possible Martin is weaker even than you.

> *TOM moves to allow ARTHUR his exit.*

I guess I have a type.

> *TOM stands still and the apartment around him disappears. He is now in a park, in the wide open and in the bright sunshine. It's possible that we only now realize that each of the settings before this was small, cramped, and shadowy. From off:*

TAMMY *(laughing)* No, that's not what it means.

TODD Yes, that's exactly what it means. The problem is, you don't understand the government.

TAMMY And you do?

TODD Yes, I do. It used to be called unemployment insurance. Now it's called *employment* insurance.

> *TAMMY and TODD enter. She pushes a baby carriage. TOM recognizes them.*

TAMMY Wait, slow down, it's called what now?

TODD Employment insurance.

TAMMY Uh huh...

TODD   It *was* called unemployment insurance, and you paid into it when you were working, so that you were, like *insured* in case you ever became unemployed. Right?

TAMMY   Uh huh…

TODD   But then they changed it so that you're insured, if you don't have a job, you collect it as insurance against *ever getting* a job. That's why it's called Employment Insurance.

TAMMY   I see.

TODD   So as long as I'm collecting EI, I'm not allowed to get a job.

TAMMY   Oh. Okay.

TODD   Really?

TAMMY   NO, YOU STUPID WAD, NOT REALLY. YOU'RE GETTING A JOB.

TODD   Your problem is, you don't understand the government.

TAMMY   Oh my God. How do you remember to breathe all day long?

TODD sees TOM.

TODD   Hey, sir? Sir?

TOM   Hello Todd.

TODD   Uh, hello.

TOM   You've had a baby.

TODD   *(peering into the carriage)* Holy shit, is that what that thing is?

TOM   Congratulations.

TODD   Right on.

TAMMY is focused on the baby carriage and doesn't look at TOM.

TOM   You don't remember me?

TODD   Uh, no. Sorry.

TOM   It's okay.

TODD   Did you sell me weed in high school?

TOM   No.

TODD   Acid? Shrooms?

TOM   No. It's okay.

TODD   Tam? You remember this guy?

She finally glances at TOM.

TAMMY   Should I?

TOM   No. Not at all.

TODD   Right on. Do you know where the swings are around here?

TAMMY   We don't need swings. She's asleep.

TODD   We'll wake her up. Do you know where the swings are around here?

TOM   No. I don't.

TODD   But, like, there are swings here, right? I remember swings.

TOM   I don't know.

TODD   Kind of a bullshit park without swings, though, right?

TOM   I don't know.

TAMMY   It's okay. Thank you. *(to TODD)* We don't need swings.

TODD   Like fuck we don't. If we get home and she wakes up, she'll be like: "What the fuck! What happened to the swings?" You don't want to put up with that shit.

TAMMY   She's three months old. When she wakes up she'll be like: "Hey, I shit myself and where's that tit I like?"

> *As they cross, a baby's sun hat falls from the stroller. TAMMY and TODD don't notice.*

You're the one who likes the swings.

TODD   Everybody likes the swings. I'm just man enough to admit it.

> *They exit. TOM notices the hat and crosses to it. He looks after TODD and TAMMY. He turns away and exits. Blackout.*

ACT TWO SCENE ONE

*The Northrop Frye quote from the top of the play has, during
the interval, reasserted itself somewhere.* TODD *enters.*

TODD   That was harsh, right? The gay guys? That guy loses
everything, his boyfriend fucks right off, and suddenly, like,
he can't even bring himself to do the thing with the baby's
hat? Harsh.

They aren't coming back, by the way. That's it for them. From
here on out, it's just me. Just you and me... So...

What's the right thing to do? How do you know when you're
happy?

My experience of adulthood is that the answers to those
questions—what the fuck should I do, am I happy right
now—show up so long after the questions get asked, it's not
even funny. Adulthood is about waiting for the answers to
arrive. It's about standing there like a friggin' dork, waiting.

Fortunately for me, I came to my adulthood already with a philosophy in place. The philosophy of: what the fuck. If you can eat that, have inside you the philosophy of what the fuck, then, well, it's great for helping you with the ridiculous waiting that is your adulthood.

Balls. I forgot my little towel. I'm supposed to be out here with one thing and I forgot it. Oh well. What the fuck. Can I have a towel, someone?

A beat.

And now, we wait.

A pause.

I have a whole thing about fairness, about the whole idea of fairness, but, like, I don't think I should start it without the towel, so...

TOM *from Act One enters with a towel.*

Oh, shit, thanks, I— Hey! Look! It's that guy! Dude. That was harsh.

TOM *waits.*

Uh. Thanks, dude.

TOM *exits.*

Seriously, though, that's it for him. Like, you might see him out here humping furniture around, but that's it.

TODD *hands the towel, in the flow of the following, to someone in the front row of the house.*

Okay. Fairness. Here's the thing I want to discuss: sometimes I don't get what you get. People are, like, "How come I don't get this," or, like, "Look at what that dude got!" Which I never got. Fairness. Fairness is like the thing, the one thing people, like, my sister? She has a fucking cat? But I never expected a cat. I never went, like, "Where's my fucking cat," you know? And it's not fair that her cat pees and even though it's her cat, I have to smell it, but what the fuck? What's the behaviour after that? I go to her and go, "Fuck, your cat makes the house reek. Make your cat produce smell-less pee"? Like, I mean, that's not possible.

I don't need to tell you that. You're adults. But it's like, like, I *do*. People need to be reminded that grade one is grade one, and the world is the world, and there's a fuckin' difference. I mean, so, I don't live there anymore, right? With my sister? That's the only thing I can do, because, like, smell-less pee hasn't been invented yet. And I can only control myself, not the pee from the cat.

I mean, like… I mean… I'm a guy, right? I'm a guy. And I go around, just, like, doing things, like other people, and suddenly this happens or that happens, some crazy horrible bullshit, and I'm like: "Whoa! That was some crazy horrible bullshit, right there." Like most people. But then, and this is where I feel I differ from most people, most people then go: "That's not fair." You know? Which is like, now you've got two problems: the crazy horrible shit that happened, and the whole, like, fairness problem, which isn't even a real problem, just a sort of myth, the myth of fairness, and it just makes the world, it just, doubles the problems.

Fairness, you know what fairness is? It's—

BRIAN from Act One enters holding a towel.

Oh. Uh, hi. I got one.

BRIAN hesitates.

Okay, no, here, thanks.

TODD goes to BRIAN, takes the towel. BRIAN exits.

That guy. Like, what was his—*ugh*.

In the following, TODD gives the second towel to another audience member.

Everybody was like: "Why do you get to narrate this part?" and I was like: "Shut up." And they were all "But blah blah blah, if you get to then everybody should!" Which is exactly what I'm talking about. I'm the motherfucking narrator. So suck it, bitches.

Fairness, the need for it, is just fear. That's all. And you have to just wait that shit out.

Am I happy. What should I do.

He waits. The apartment begins to assemble around him. The Northrop Frye quote fades and is replaced by the following:

> Freedom is a chilly virtue: it is not justice, equality or a quiet life; it is merely freedom.
> —Isaiah Berlin

TODD notices this, reads. He turns to the audience.

I've never found these things particularly helpful.

The quote fades, the baby, off, squeals, and TODD steps into the scene.

TODD and TAMMY's apartment. It's kind of terrible and small. The front door is wide open and there's a piece of paper tacked to it. TODD stands in front of LISA, who is trying to tie a tie on TODD. The baby is crying, off.

LISA   Why not?

TODD   Because.

LISA   Because why.

TODD   Because why? Holy shit, Lisa. Because I'm married?

LISA   I know, but why else.

TODD   That doesn't do it for you? My whole marriage that I'm in?

LISA   No. Because I know you want it. Marriage or no marriage.

TODD   How about because you're supposed to be best friends with my best friend, which is my wife. Which is the lady I married, okay? Is it your like life goal to become the skankiest person in Canada?

LISA   Nothing's gonna happen. I just want to hear you say you want it.

TODD   Fucking no.

LISA   But, like, are you happy?

TODD   You know what—

        A pause.

        Do you even know how to do one of these?

LISA   Not really.

TODD   Jesus. I knew it.

LISA   But maybe I do. Maybe I'm learning as I do it. It's just a knot.

TODD   Look, if it was just a knot, everyone could do it.

TAMMY   *(from off)* Todd!

TODD   Yeah?

TAMMY   Do you know where her soother is?

TODD   I don't even know what that is.

TAMMY   It's the thing you put in her mouth when she's, like, crying. I want to find it in case she starts, like, crying.

TODD   I hate to tell you, sweetie, but she's already cry—

TAMMY   *(appearing in a door)* I KNOW SHE'S FUCKING CRYING! DO YOU KNOW WHERE HER SOOTHER IS?

TODD   I really don't.

TAMMY   Jesus, Lisa, do you have to crawl on top of him every time I leave the room?

LISA   I'm doing his knot.

TAMMY   *(as she goes)* Leave him alone. He has to go and get a job now.

LISA   Almost done.

TODD   No you're not. Forget it. I'll go without the tie. I mean, if my wearing a tie is the difference between me getting a job and not getting a job, then that's so fucked I can't stand it. Aw, shit.

> *He sees the paper on the door and pulls it down. He folds it and shoves it in a pocket.*

It's like they think that we just forget to pay our rent. Like putting a notice on the door about how long until we get kicked out is going to make the money just appear like a magic show. Like I'm that guy frozen in a block of ice for two months or something. And when I get out, I crap rent money. Don't tell Tam. She'll shit herself.

TAMMY   *(from off)* TODD!

TODD   She already is. But on different topics.

TAMMY   *(entering with the soother)* I found it. Do you know where I found it?

TODD   I don't even know what it is.

TAMMY   I found it in the garbage.

TODD   Wow. Fucking mommy brain, right?

TAMMY   I DIDN'T PUT IT THERE. It was wrapped in a Kit Kat wrapper inside a sock. What's the matter with you?

TODD   Well, I don't think she should be using that. It's not right. It's lying to her. It's all nipple and no milk. It's cheating, am I right?

LISA   No.

TODD   No, but, am I right? It's teaching her cheating.

TAMMY   It's called a soother. Do you know why?

TODD   'Cause it's soothing?

TAMMY   'Cause it's soothing. She likes it. It makes her feel good. It makes her sleep.

TODD   Sure, but under false pretenses.

        GEORGE *Ambali appears at the door. He's in his early thirties, Somali.*

TAMMY   So what! Don't you want her to sleep?

TODD   It's great when she sleeps. Hey! Let's all go to sleep.

TAMMY   Not you. You have to go for that job interview. So put that tie on.

TAMMY exits.

TODD   Balls.

> *TODD regards the tie. He puts it around his neck and starts to fiddle with it.*

I never should have undone it after the wedding.

LISA   Maybe not.

> *TODD and the tie for a long beat. The baby stops crying.*

Todd?

TODD   No.

LISA   Todd?

TODD   No, shut up, I almost got it.

LISA   There's a black dude at the door.

TODD   Twenty-two dollars for this friggin' thing. For an *accessory*.

LISA   Todd?

TODD   Like, we don't have all the main shit of life yet, and here I am, fucking around with an accessory.

LISA   There's a black guy at the door.

> *TODD looks up.*

TODD   Hey.

GEORGE   Hello.

TODD   Do you know how to do one of these fucking things?

A beat.

GEORGE   Hello.

TODD   Hello. Do you know how to do one of these fucking things?

A beat.

GEORGE   I am George. George Ambali.

TODD   Awesome. I have to put this on. Do you know how I do that?

GEORGE smiles.

My name is Todd.

GEORGE   George Ambali.

TODD   Yes. Your English sort of blows, doesn't it?

GEORGE   English... is... my... no.

TODD   Okay. Right on. That's okay.

GEORGE   I am living... this apartment.

He gestures to the apartment next door.

TODD   Oh, okay. I'm Todd? Todd Going? I am living... this apartment.

GEORGE   Okay.

TODD   Okay. C'mon in, George.

GEORGE   No, I...

He gestures toward his apartment.

TODD   No, c'mon in. Have a seat.

GEORGE   But, I...

TODD   It's okay. I have to go to a job thing. So instead let's get to know our new neighbour. George.

GEORGE   But.

TODD   Dude. I insist.

> *He brings* GEORGE *into the room, sits him on the couch.*

LISA   I'm Lisa. Li-sa.

GEORGE   Lisa.

TODD   Skank.

GEORGE   Skank.

> GEORGE *shakes* LISA*'s hand.*

TODD   So, like, George, where are you from?

GEORGE   I am this apartment. The apartment.

TODD   That apartment?

GEORGE   *(a great relief)* Yes! That apartment.

LISA   How the fuck did you get that apartment? I've been trying to get in this building for two years.

> GEORGE *smiles at her.*

TODD   They must have a no-skank policy. George. George. This is Ca-na-da. Right?

GEORGE   Yes. Canada. Very, very good.

TODD   But where are *you* from?

GEORGE   Oh! Yes. I am Somali.

TODD   So, but, where are you *from*?

GEORGE   I am Somali.

TODD   I know, but... fuck it. Way to go, George. I bet it was a real pain in the ass getting here.

   TAMMY enters.

TAMMY   Todd, what are you doing here? Your interview is in twenty minutes.

TODD   Yeah, I know, but if I can't get this fucking tie on, what's the point, you know?

TAMMY   TODD, I SWEAR TO FUCKING CHRIST, IF YOU DON'T GET YOUR FUCKING ASS OUT THE DOOR AND GET A JOB, I'M GOING TO—who is this?

   GEORGE is terrified of TAMMY.

TODD   This is George. He moved in next door. He's from somewhere.

TAMMY   Hello. You moved in next door? To that apartment next door?

GEORGE   Yes!

TAMMY   I applied for us to move there when Mrs. Whatshername died. How did you get that place? Are you sure it's your apartment?

   GEORGE produces a piece of paper.

TODD   It's okay, George. I don't like that place any worse than this place.

TAMMY   *(reading)* It's cheaper, fucknose.

   The government gave it to him.

LISA   What?

TAMMY   The government gave it to him. Fuck me. Because he's new. Look.

She gives LISA *the paper.*

LISA   Well, shit. He gets free rent for like a year.

GEORGE   Asylum.

TODD   Way to go, dude. Where do I sign up?

TAMMY   Do you understand that many, many people wanted that apartment? That we wanted that apartment? Do you understand that?

GEORGE   I am... I...

TODD   It's okay. *(to* TAMMY*)* Give the guy a break. He just got here.

TAMMY   I know, but shit. Well. Whatever. You better get out of here.

TODD   Yeah. I was gonna tell you? My appointment was for 11:30, not 2:30.

TAMMY   IT WHAT?

TODD   Yeah, like, I don't know how it happened—

TAMMY   TODD!

TODD   Hold onto your balls, George.

A pause.

TAMMY   Todd. We have thirteen dollars. We can't eat at your mum's every night. We're a family now, okay? We got married, and now we have to live. We have to live, Todd, okay?

TODD   Okay.

TAMMY   I don't want to be a bitch.

TODD   I don't want to be an asshole. But as long as I'm an asshole, you have to be a bitch.

TAMMY   That's right. Now get the fuck out of here. Go see if they'll still see you.

TODD   Okay. Hey, George, listen up. I need to go to like Ajax or Etobicoke or something. I have to see about getting a job

GEORGE   Job?

TODD   That's right. I'm the man and I need a job. Want to come? I can show you around.

GEORGE   Yes. Okay.

      GEORGE stands. The apartment disappears.

TODD   *(to us)* I understand, right? I understand. I get that part. I need to get a job. But I have this habit: my whole life, I made people tell me things three or four times before I do something. Because you would be amazed how often people say: "Do this" when they don't give a fuck if you do it or not. It's a thing I've noticed. People, like, I don't know, they like to tell people what to do. It's human nature: the need to be the bully. And the way to combat that is to make people tell you three or four times if they want you to do a thing. Because if they don't really, if they just want to exercise their powers, then they give up after a couple of tries. Only people who really really want you to do something tell you a bunch of times. Which makes me kind of not the best employee, when I do have a job. But fuck it. I'm trying to correct a part of our inbreeding, humanity's long-term inbreeding.

      PETE Artless opens a door.

(to us) I can guarantee you, this will be quick. *(to* PETE*)* No fuckin' way. *Eleven* thirty?

> TODD *goes through the door with* PETE. GEORGE *sits in a chair, waiting. It's possible he resembles* ARTHUR *from Act One, waiting quietly for* TOM. *Time passes. The office door opens and* TODD *walks out with* PETE.

Okay, so, that's great. I've always been good with pop. 'Member Fresca? Ever get that shit in your eye?

PETE Okay, well, as long as you're okay with lifting shit.

TODD It's like what I do best. So, like, full-time?

PETE Friggin' right, full-time. From like right now. I need to get a buttload of cases to a Giant Tiger in Moncton.

TODD Okay. I don't know where that is. I know they have a hockey team.

PETE Yeah, it's okay. I just need you to put the labels on the bottles, and put the bottles into cases, and put the cases on the truck.

TODD Right on.

PETE Okay. But, Todd.

TODD Pop guy?

PETE Call me Pete. Do you drink?

TODD Not this shit.

PETE Not pop. Booze. I have to ask.

TODD Well, sure. Wait. Is beer considered booze?

PETE So, like, I'm. This is. Wow, this is funny, I've never hired anyone before. Look, Todd? I'm in a program, okay?

TODD   Right on.

PETE   I have a drinking problem.

TODD   Oh! Right on.

PETE   So I can't have people around me drinking, okay?

TODD   No, right on.

PETE   Okay.

TODD   Okay?

PETE   Okay. I mean... Okay.

TODD   All right! Woo hoo!

PETE   Can I help you?

TODD   That's George. Hey! George! I'm this guy's first fuckin' employee!

> TODD *goes to* GEORGE, GEORGE *stands.*

GEORGE   Did you... job?

TODD   Fucking right I jobbed. That's what I'm saying. This is my new boss, Alcoholic Pete.

GEORGE   Hello.

TODD   Show him your papers. The papers.

> GEORGE *is confused.* TODD *pats him down, finds the papers.*

Look at this.

> PETE *reads the papers.*

He was getting politically fucked. They gave him this apartment. We were in line for it, but—

PETE Shit. Hey. Do *you* need a job?

GEORGE A job, yes.

PETE This says that I can… uh. Shit. Todd?

TODD Yes?

PETE This says that the government will subsidize his pay for the first ten months. Did you know that?

TODD No. He gets what? George! You hit the friggin' jackpot, didn't you?

PETE So. Shit. Todd?

TODD *(to us)* So that was how George got a job. Or like half a job. Pete hires me part-time, George part-time, and it's like he's paying one full-time human being, but getting two. My new boss is wily. His pop tastes like cat pee, but he's wily.

The apartment reappears, and TAMMY *nurses the baby.*

He was gonna give the whole thing to George, but I told him that George's English sucks, which is true, but that I can translate for him, which sort of isn't.

TAMMY So how many hours?

TODD No, like full-time. But only paid for part-time.

TAMMY *(to the baby, softly)* We can't live on that, can we, sweetie?

A pause.

Can we.

TODD   Can we what? Are you talking to me?

TAMMY   There was a thing on the door.

> *A beat.*

So, Todd. What are we gonna do?

TODD   I know, right?

> *A pause.*

TAMMY   Can you take her? I'm going to bed.

TODD   It's five o'clock.

TAMMY   You should get a job telling the time.

> TODD *takes the baby and* TAMMY *exits.*

TODD   *(to us)* My point was, it's not normal to go to bed at five o'clock. It's also not normal to fall asleep standing in line at the friggin' Sobeys. But say that to a doctor and he goes, like, "What do you want from me, she's tired, she's a mum, get the fuck out of my office"—like, once you notice the human's inbred need to bully, you see it everywhere, am I right? So, okay, what do I know, I'm just a guy in a marriage, okay, sorry to waste your time.

> *The apartment begins to change to* GEORGE's *apartment. Baby things, open suitcases overflowing with clothes; it's crowded.*

I don't know if you've ever been evicted, but, really, all you need to know about the experience is, like, right there in the word. Evicted. Eeeee-*vic*-ted.

> GEORGE *enters.* TODD *talks to the baby.*

Hey! Who's that? Who's that? That's George.

GEORGE   Tammy says dinner.

> *GEORGE takes the baby.*

TODD   Okay. George?

> *GEORGE stops.*

I'm the head of my family, and some day I'll start acting like it. So, but, thanks for having us. In your government apartment.

GEORGE   It's good, Toddy. Come.

> *GEORGE goes.*

TODD   So far, being an adult seems mostly about shame.

> *A beat. PETE's pop operation assembles.*

But, what the fuck. That's okay. For now. I get there's a whole lot of things I don't get, that I can't do yet, that are complete friggin' mysteries to me but also happen to be my life now. So I say, what the fuck. Give me a minute, I'll get there. I'll figure it out. You see, the thing about me is, I have this awesome ability to—

GEORGE   *Qado.*

TODD   Oh. Hang on. What?

> *TODD enters the scene. GEORGE and PETE are soaking bottles of pop in a tub of water, then carefully peeling off the labels, which are upside down, and putting them back on right side up. TODD sits and takes up a bottle. GEORGE accomplishes this task roughly three times faster than TODD. The colour of the pop in the bottles is frightening.*

GEORGE   Qado.

TODD   Qa-do?

GEORGE   Qado.

TODD   Lunch?

GEORGE   Lunch.

TODD   Right on. So, like, what?

GEORGE   What what.

TODD   What was lunch?

GEORGE   Rice. Vegetables. *Maraq*, which is stew. Things.

TODD   Right on.

GEORGE   Spaghetti.

TODD   What!?

GEORGE   Yes!

TODD   No fucking way.

GEORGE   Fucking yes. Is called *baasto*.

TODD   African fucking spaghetti!

PETE   Shut up, okay? This shit is late.

TODD   Meatballs?

GEORGE   Sorry?

TODD   Meatballs? Like, balls of meat? On the spaghetti?

PETE   Shut up, okay?

TODD   No, but, aren't you, don't you want to know?

PETE   I guess.

GEORGE   No balls of meat.

TODD   Oh.

GEORGE   Goat, um, goat's liver. Sometimes.

TODD   On spaghetti?

GEORGE   With, yes.

TODD   Fuck. That's weak.

PETE   Aren't you glad you asked?

TODD   Pete, yes I am. I'm glad I asked, even if the answer is fucking sickening. I'm expanding my shit by talking with George. I'm expanding my shit, and he gets English practise. George, it's not your fault you ate goat balls on spaghetti. Those days are over, my friend.

GEORGE   Yes. Good.

        A pause. They work.

        But I like goat.

TODD   Yes. And that's not your fault.

GEORGE   I make goat good.

TODD   In this country, George, goat is only good for one thing. And I don't even know what that is.

GEORGE   I make baasto, goat on top, best of all of us. Better than mother. Better than wife. It is my dish.

TODD   What wife? Your wife?

> *GEORGE is quiet.*

What the fuck, dude?

PETE   Where is she?

GEORGE She is not... here.

TODD   No shit. If she was, she could help us with these fucking labels. Sorry about these labels, by the way.

PETE   Are you making money to bring her?

GEORGE No.

> *A pause.*

TODD   So, like, she, is she? Did she? Get?

> *GEORGE says nothing.*

(to PETE) There's like this fucked up three-way clusterfuck war over there. They made a movie about it.

> *A beat.*

GEORGE We had a baby. Like yours. Small.

TODD   Aw, fuck. No way.

PETE   George, what happened?

TODD   He doesn't have to tell, you don't have to tell, if it's like, too—

GEORGE Men of my religion. They fight the government. But there is no real government, you know? They fight. And I am, I say no to leaving my home to fight with my brothers. The government men come, I am not fighting against them, so they say I must fight with them. Against the religious people, my brothers. I have no choice, they make it clear. I go away. I fight for the government. I escape, I come back. The religious people have been there, they have taken my town. And I am a government soldier, they believe. My house is burnt. My wife, gone. My baby, gone.

PETE   Gone? So you don't know if they, maybe they—

GEORGE   No. Sorry, my English. I mean they were... there, you know? In my house.

TODD   Fuck me.

GEORGE   I go to Ethiopia. I walk.

> *A pause.*

PETE   George, you know what that was? You know how you got here? That was God. You know that?

GEORGE   Yes. Please. I don't have... I am not any more religious.

TODD   No fucking kidding.

PETE   George. Yes. It was God. You were spared and it was God that did it.

GEORGE   Well...

PETE   It was. It was.

TODD   Ease up there, Christy. Where's this God shit coming from?

PETE   George, listen to me. After, you can tell me to fuck off if you want. Your life. It's a gift. You were spared. You have to see it that way. God spared your life, so it's a gift. Otherwise, what's the alternative? The alternative is that there's absolutely no point. The alternative is, all of life is pain and accidents and stupidity and then you die. Do you think your wife, and your baby, would want that? Would they want you to live your life thinking that? You, here, alive, in this place, it's a gift.

GEORGE   To be here.

PETE   It's God's gift.

GEORGE   Yes.

PETE   George, I want you to come with me. Right now.

GEORGE   Go?

PETE   There's a lot of people who'd like to meet you. Yes. At my church.

GEORGE   Now?

TODD   You've got a church?

PETE   Right now.

TODD   You're what, alcoholic and also religious?

PETE   It's a blessing, George. A friggin', honest-to-God blessing.

TODD   Well, that explains the little hairy dude on these labels.

PETE and GEORGE rise.

PETE   We'll be back. C'mon, George.

They leave TODD. He starts to clean up as he talks to us.

TODD   Which is how George got religion. Now, I'm not sure how to feel about that. I mean, here's a guy, fresh off a boat, basically fucked, and they're on him like vultures. But are they like vultures? I mean, I don't get it, but holy fuck, the list of things I don't get is quite extensive. And, I mean, he wouldn't do it if it didn't do something for him. He must get something out of it. Maybe if I'm him, dead people make up most of my family at this point, maybe a church is like the only place large enough to hold what that's like.

Anyway, the point is, these labels come on a big sheet, and they go in the machine this way. *(He gestures.)* Not the other way. Little tip for ya.

> TODD *goes. The apartment assembles.* TAMMY *is asleep on the couch, the baby asleep as well, on her chest.* GEORGE *enters wearing* TODD's *tie. He pauses when he sees* TAMMY *and her child.* GEORGE *regards them for a long time.*

> *Finally, the baby fusses and* TAMMY *wakes up. Sees* GEORGE *watching them. She sits, looking for the soother.*

GEORGE   Tammy. Maybe I… help with dinner? Or—

TAMMY   I don't… What time is it? Oh, God. Something's happening to me.

GEORGE   You are sick?

TAMMY   I don't know what's happening to me.

GEORGE   Tammy. Let me help you.

TAMMY   I don't know. I'm just. What am I doing? No. Okay.

> TAMMY *rises to put the baby down.* TODD *enters the apartment.*

TODD   Hey Tam. What's for—

> *But* TAMMY *leaves.*

Hey! What happened to you? I had to load out for Sarnia all by myself.

GEORGE   Todd.

TODD   George.

GEORGE   Do you have God in your heart?

TODD   Aw, fuck. Look, okay? It's great, you know, that you go to Pete's church and everything, but asking other people about that shit, it's like—

GEORGE   Todd.

TODD   Here, talking about religion like that, trying to get people to sign up, it's—

GEORGE   Toddy.

TODD   It's, you know what it is, George? I'm serious. It's a sin. An embarrassing sin, and you need to stop embarrassing yourself with that shit, and also stop sinning.

GEORGE   Todd. I'm kidding.

TODD   You, what?

GEORGE   I'm joking. I'm jerking you.

TODD   You're— Holy fuck! Fantastic!

> *TODD dissolves in laughter. TAMMY returns.*

C'mere. Listen to this. His first fucking English joke. Do it to her.

GEORGE   I was baptized this afternoon.

> *A beat.*

TODD   Yeah, that one's not as funny. Do the other one.

TAMMY   When, just today?

A knock at the door. TODD goes.

GEORGE   Yes.

TAMMY   That's nice, George. I'm glad.

LISA enters.

TODD   Hey. Leese. C'mere. *(to GEORGE)* Do the other one, the first one. To her.

GEORGE   Lisa. Do you have God in your heart?

A beat, then LISA bursts into laughter.

TODD   I know, right?

LISA   Good one. You all set?

GEORGE   Yes.

TODD   What's...?

LISA   George and I are going out for dinner.

A beat, TODD is thrown.

TODD   Really? *(to GEORGE)* Really?

GEORGE   Really. We are going for pan...

LISA   Panzarotti.

GEORGE   Panzarotti. Baked or fried.

LISA   How do you like that, asslick?

TODD   I'm like, hasn't the guy been through enough?

TAMMY   Have fun. Congratulations on your baptism.

They go. TODD *is silent.*

What.

TODD   What?

TAMMY   Fuck you. Look at that. You're jealous.

TODD   Of what, of them?

TAMMY   Yes. Yes you are. Jesus!

TODD   Well, let me ask you this: are we having panzarotti for dinner tonight?

TAMMY   No.

TODD   Then, fuck yeah I'm jealous.

TAMMY   You can't stand it. You like to have all your women where you can reach them.

TODD   No, I don't, it's just... what if he turns her into one of them?

TAMMY   One of them? You know, I used to go to church when I was little.

TODD   Yeah, okay.

TAMMY   It actually means something.

TODD   Okay. Okay. Never mind. Fuck. I wish them a long and happy life with Jesus.

    A pause.

How are you like feeling, and everything? Did you...

    A pause.

Did you get up to anything today?

TAMMY   What do you mean?

TODD   I mean, uh, did you get up today?

>   *A pause.*

>   Hey. I made a new flavour. You know what you get when you mix lemon-lime and cranberry?

TAMMY   What.

TODD   You basically get your boss yelling at you for a half an hour.

TAMMY   You told me that one yesterday.

TODD   I know, I'm just, trying to…

>   *A pause.*

TAMMY   Todd?

TODD   Yeah.

TAMMY   I… I can't… I don't feel like…

TODD   Tam. It's okay. Whatever it is. We'll fix it.

TAMMY   But. What are we doing?

TODD   We're doing the thing we said.

TAMMY   I used to believe it. Now…

TODD   Now what? You don't? You don't believe it?

TAMMY   No, I, I just.

TODD   Because, like, belief is all it is. It's all belief.

TAMMY   No, okay.

TODD   What.

TAMMY   Just, okay. Stop.

     A pause.

TODD   I'm hungry.

TAMMY   You're always hungry.

TODD   I don't know what to tell you. I'm hungry. It's possible I'm experiencing a growth spurt.

TAMMY   Jesus.

     A beat.

TODD   So, can you...?

TAMMY   Can I what, *make you something*?

TODD   Well, yeah. As long as you're up.

TAMMY   Sure thing, sweetie. Like, an omelette?

TODD   Right on.

     She leaves.

The thing is, it's completely possible that I'm experiencing some sort of growth spurt. Like, I'm that young? Both me and Tammy are still so young that, like, our doctor? Our new one? We went because Tammy is having feelings, of like, and like I said the first guy goes, "Get out of my office," so we went to another one, a lady, and she goes, the doctor goes—

     TAMMY returns with an egg. She whips it at TODD, hitting him in the head. She goes. TODD retrieves the towels from various audience members and cleans himself off, getting a good look at the audience as he does so.

Let's, let's try to keep in mind, okay, because I can hear you out there, going, whatever, making decisions about her. I don't mind things like this. Like, these days, her being a bitch is way, way better than her usual thing of just sleeping. Our new doctor told us that her thing is a legitimate thing, okay? Like mood and sleeping and all about that, and, like, she told us everything about it except for how to fucking fix it. She's like: "You just have to fucking go through it." She's like: "It's probably temporary." And I'm all, so, okay, I'll wait, just one more thing I don't get but I might someday. Meanwhile, my wife, my friend here, she's fading into a ghost, a ghost that won't even fight with me anymore. So, like, you're sitting out there and you're all, "What a bitch, she threw an egg," and I'm like, "She threw an egg, awesome."

A beat.

The pressure is enormous. That should be in the wedding vows: "…I now pronounce you—oh, by the way, the pressure's enormous—man and friggin' wife."

LISA and GEORGE return. GEORGE has tomato sauce all over his shirt and TODD's tie.

How was it? Which way'd you go, George, baked or fried?

GEORGE   Fried.

TODD   Fuckin' right, fried. You?

LISA   I had a salad.

TODD   Nice. Baked or fried?

GEORGE   Thank you, Lisa.

LISA   No problem. Happy baptism.

GEORGE   Todd. I think I…

TODD   I know. It's okay.

GEORGE   I fucked your tie.

TODD   It looks better that way. Fuckin' thing.

GEORGE   Good night, Toddy.

TODD   Night, George Ambali the Somali.

GEORGE   *(shaking LISA's hand)* Good night.

LISA   See ya, George.

> *He goes. A pause.*

> Did he tell you about his family?

TODD   Yeah.

> *A pause.*

LISA   You looked funny. When we left.

TODD   Yeah, okay. Lisa?

LISA   Todd?

TODD   The thing is, you know, it's a lot of pressure. And it's not going so good, not all the time, and I don't really know what to do about it, and, like, there you are, standing there, and, okay, I remember, okay, it was nice, you were nice, but that's not... I can't...

LISA   I know.

TODD   Like, as the pressure mounts, I won't always have the brain to go: "Stop it, Lisa, fuck off," you know? At some point, things are worse, and I'm, and through fear, I'll do it. And it'll be gross. So, look, I'm, like, begging you. Don't, okay? Because I won't always have the powers to withstand you.

LISA   I know.

    A pause.

The heart wants what it wants.

TODD   What? That's what you say to me? Holy fuck. That's like the stupidest, like, I'm not intelligent, okay, like AT ALL, and even I know, EVEN I KNOW, that's a stupid argument. The heart wants what it wants. Yeah, okay, and the balls want what they want, and your asshole often wants something too. I HAVE A SITUATION. Can your fuckin' heart wrap its fuckin' head around that?

LISA   No, I don't think so. Sorry.

TODD   Jesus motherfucking—

    A beat.

LISA   You want to know why?

TODD   Do I fucking look like I want to know why?

LISA   A little bit.

TODD   Fuckin', I... please. Lisa. Please.

    A beat; she regards him.

LISA   Okay. See ya.

    She goes. A moment of TODD *in genuine distress.* TAMMY *rounds a corner; she was obviously listening.* TODD *notices her.*

TODD   Can we like, please ban her?

    A pause.

TAMMY You know what, Todd? She's my only friend. And I'm, okay, don't take this the wrong way, but I'm lonely.

TODD Yeah. Okay.

> *They look at each other for a moment. She goes. The apartment goes too.*

"It's probably temporary. You just have to wait and get through it." Literally, the new doctor turns to me at that moment and looks right at me and tells me *how* to wait, and *how* to get through it, then that's some actual doctoring. Tell me how to stand over here and just wait. Tell me. Tell me how, and I'm good.

> *A pause.*

But, so, okay. What the fuck.

PETE Todd!

> *We're now at work.*

There you are. Where's George?

TODD Not sure. It's his break, so I'm gonna guess he's praying. Or maybe just thinking about praying. Or, like, writing down what he's gonna pray next.

PETE Fuck you.

TODD I'm just saying, that guy was more fun before you dragged him off to, I mean, I was kinda moulding him in my own image there, for a while.

PETE You see this? You know what this is?

TODD A page of paper? Of some sort?

PETE This is the motherlode, brother.

GEORGE enters.

George! We did it! You did it!

GEORGE   No way.

PETE   Yes.

GEORGE   No way!

PETE   Yes!

GEORGE and PETE embrace. TODD waits, smiling.

TODD   What.

GEORGE   Toddy!

GEORGE embraces TODD.

TODD   Yeah, okay. Okay. Great. What?

GEORGE   Walmart!

PETE   This is our first order from Walmart Canada.

TODD   No way. And it's big?

PETE   Friggin' enormous. I sent George. He sold it! He closed the deal. George closed the deal.

GEORGE   Well...

PETE   The buyer, we met him one day at East Gate. George was up reading one Sunday, and—

GEORGE   My English, you know, it was, what, Matthew 6:31—

TODD   Sure.

GEORGE   "…What shall we eat? Or what shall we drink? Or wherewithal shall we be clothed? For after all these things do the Gentiles seek." And I said "gentlies" instead of "Gentiles."

PETE   "…do the Gentlies seek."

GEORGE   I said: "…do the Gentlies seek." And I just, I couldn't get past it. I keep looking at the word. Gently? Gentlies? And I said it over and over, and then I just stopped.

PETE   The place went quiet. Nobody knew what to do. How to help. George's English, it's, you know, amazing, but, and—

GEORGE   And a man stood up, and recited the entire passage from memory.

PETE   It's about prosperity, Matthew 6:31.

TODD   Sure.

GEORGE   "…What shall we eat? Or what shall we drink? Or wherewithal shall we be clothed? For after all these things do the Gentiles seek. But seek ye first the kingdom of God, and his righteousness; and all these things shall be added unto you." And then the man said to me: "And that's my wish for you, here, in your new home. All the things you have need of. I wish you prosperity."

PETE   Everyone clapped. Everyone cheered.

TODD   In church?

GEORGE   It was, maybe the greatest moment of my life here.

PETE   And the man, it turns out, is a buyer for Walmart Canada, and we talked after, and then I sent George to his office to pitch our pop.

GEORGE   I said: "I'm here to see you about that prosperity we discussed."

PETE   Really? You said that? That's great!

        Fuck me, look at that. Four thousand cases. And that's just the first order. I have to hire more people.

TODD   Damn right. People I can boss around.

PETE   Well, Todd, I need you to be, like, loading, it's what you do best, so…

TODD   Yeah, but, new people, they have to be trained, but, so, like, I'm that guy, right?

PETE   Well, Todd, we'll talk about it.

TODD   Hey. Come on. You can't leave us off the friggin' bus now that you're on your way to Honeytown.

PETE   We'll talk. You'd better finish packing for the night order.

TODD   Fuck. All right. C'mon, George. I got a new game I can show you, but you have to know how to balance a bottle on your forehead.

PETE   He has to… he's coming with me.

        A beat.

TODD   No, sure.

        PETE and GEORGE exit.

        The thing was, because he fucked up my tie, he had to go out and buy a bunch of new ones. So, like, there you go. From "Hello. I am going from Africa," to "Hey, Todd, stop fucking around and put that shit on the truck."

        And, like, okay. Okay. But what the fuck.

        A beat.

I wasn't here for this part.

> TODD *leaves. A moment of quiet, then* TAMMY *walks on. The apartment assembles around her. As soon as there's somewhere to sit, she sits, holds her face, and cries.* GEORGE *enters and watches her. He's wearing a tie now. She sees him and they have a moment, held in each other's eyes, where she weeps unashamedly.* GEORGE *crosses to her, lifts her to her feet, and hugs her. Eventually, she breaks this, looks at him, and exits.* GEORGE *waits. She returns, wiping her face with a diaper.*

TAMMY   He's making more money. We can move out of here.

> *A pause.*

GEORGE   You know, everybody here knows what happened to my family. But nobody asks what I did in the war.

> *A beat.*

You should stay as long as you want. Please.

> *He goes.* TAMMY *blows her nose into the diaper. The lights change and* TODD *and* LISA *enter;* LISA *holds the baby.*

TODD   You ready?

TAMMY   Yes. *(to* LISA*)* You gonna be okay?

LISA   Of course.

TAMMY   I don't even know why we're going. We don't have a boat.

LISA   Because you need to get out of here.

TAMMY   But, I mean, the boat show?

TODD   Yeah, but the Mothers Who Become Crazy Bitches After They Give Birth Show isn't until next week.

A beat. TODD's *joke didn't come off.*

Okay.

He ushers TAMMY *out the door.* LISA *looks at the baby. She exits. Time passes.*

GEORGE, *in a tie, enters the apartment with* PETE, *who also wears a tie. As they come in,* LISA *returns with the baby.*

GEORGE Lisa.

LISA Hey, George.

GEORGE Oh! Good! There she is.

LISA She just ate.

GEORGE Perfect.

PETE Should you change her?

GEORGE is getting the stroller.

LISA No, I just did. What's—?

GEORGE We promised Todd we'd take her out this afternoon. He wanted to have a date with Tammy.

LISA I know. She asked me to look after her.

GEORGE Oh. Todd asked me.

A beat.

We'll take her out for a while. You get some rest. Take a nap.

LISA Cool. Okay.

LISA *hands over the baby and* GEORGE *puts her in the stroller.*

She'll probably just sleep anyway.

GEORGE Yes. That's good.

  PETE finds a blanket and GEORGE tucks it around the baby.

Very nice. Okay. Enjoy your nap.

LISA Thanks.

  *Everyone exits, the men and baby out the apartment door.
The lights change. TODD and TAMMY return.*

TODD But, like, you know, they have places now, where they make
food for you, and they even fucking bring it to—

TAMMY I'm not hungry. Lisa? Lisa!

  LISA enters, sleepy.

LISA Relax. You're back early. How was the boat show?

TAMMY How is she?

TODD I took my shirt off and had my picture taken with Miss
Canada.

TAMMY She's not napping now, is she, because—

LISA No, she's out with George. They took her to I think the park.
(to TODD) Like, how many people do you need to look after one
kid? What, you don't trust me too look after your baby for a
few hours?

TODD No, I mean, sure I do.

LISA So why'd you ask George to babysit too?

TODD *(to us)* And here's where my being the narrator pays off like a
slot machine with a screwdriver shoved up it. Because, like, I

never did. *(to LISA)* Oh, fuck, right. Yeah. I forgot about George. Where'd they go? Where'd he take her?

LISA   *(to TAMMY)* So it was fun?

TAMMY   It was the boat show. It was, you know, there was one thing that—

TODD   Like, so, fuck, he took her where?

TAMMY   You know those vibrating chairs? They had one for outdoors. I tried it out, it was great. I fell asleep in it instantaneously.

TODD   And the guy goes: "You wanna get your wife out of there?" And I'm like, "No fucking way, *you* wake her up." So George took her where?

LISA   Like the park, I think.

TODD   Okay, I'm just gonna—

He heads for the door.

TAMMY   Where are you going?

TODD   I, I don't know. I'm hungry. There's nothing to eat here. So.

TAMMY   What are you doing? What's wrong?

TODD   Nothing. It's just, I haven't had anything since that bullshit thing of fish and chips for fucking eight dollars. So, I'm gonna, and you're not hungry, right, and so…

TODD, for the first time, fails to finish a sentence.

TAMMY   What. WHAT.

TODD   I fuckin', did *you* ask George to look after her?

TAMMY   I asked Lisa. What's—

TODD   Because I didn't ask George.

    A beat.

LISA   Your boss was with him.

TODD   Pete was here too?

TAMMY   LISA. WHERE'D THEY GO?

LISA   I don't, I don't—

TODD   Okay, look, I'll—

    The door opens. GEORGE and PETE return with the baby.

    Fuck!

GEORGE *(whispering)* No! She's asleep!

TODD   *(whispering)* Fuck, George! Fuck!

    TAMMY takes the baby, in the car seat, and hands her to LISA.
    LISA takes her out of the room.

    (louder now) What the fuck, George?

GEORGE How was the boat show?

TAMMY   What did you guys do?

GEORGE We took her for the afternoon.

PETE   You guys needed a break, George thought. So...

GEORGE We took her for the afternoon.

TODD   Lisa says I told you to. I didn't tell you to.

GEORGE No, I'm sorry. I know. We just wanted to give everyone a break.

TAMMY   Where did you go?

GEORGE   The park, and then to the waterfront, and then we stopped at our church.

    A beat.

    And when we were there, we had her baptized.

PETE   We had her baptized. It took ten minutes.

    A beat. TODD *lunges at* GEORGE, *knocking him down.* PETE *pulls* TODD *off.*

TODD   You motherfucking—WHY WOULD YOU DO THAT?

GEORGE   It is my duty. I love her. Not like her parents do, but it's true that I do.

TODD   But, you fuckin', you, but…

    TODD *is at a loss.*

GEORGE   Toddy. Go and look at her. She is exactly the same as this morning. And you don't believe in what we believe, so what possible difference could it make to you?

TODD   Um, I dunno, asslick, YOU STOLE HER? Maybe where you come from that's okay, but fuck, it's, it's not—

TAMMY   I think it's beautiful.

    A beat. LISA *has re-entered.*

    I think it was a beautiful thing to do.

    TAMMY *goes to* PETE, *shakes his hand.*

    Thank you.

PETE   No problem. God bless.

TAMMY goes to GEORGE. She kisses him.

TAMMY   Thank you, George.

GEORGE   It was my honour to do so.

TODD   What the fuck. Were you hoping, like did you want us to go and get her baptized?

TAMMY   It never occurred to me. It never occurred to me. *(smiling)* Isn't that sad?

GEORGE   No.

TAMMY   It is. I don't have God in my heart.

I don't have anything in my heart.

She exits. A beat, and then everyone except TODD leaves.

TODD   So, like, now, it's chaos. Now, I know nothing. Now, I'm in like a dream of utter, complete fucking, like, it's still my life, but now all the wiring is fucked and I don't know which switch turns on what light. Everything I say is wrong. Everything I do is wrong. Like, I'm not a husband. I'm some guy who lives here. She can't even look me in the eye. And I don't, like I don't know what to— *(to TAMMY, who enters)* Tell me what to do. Tell me.

TAMMY   I don't know, Todd. I just, I don't know.

TODD   Because I just, all I want is to not, I just want this to be okay, right?

TAMMY   It's not.

TODD   No fucking shit!

A pause.

Remember, remember when it was us in my room, and, I don't know, I was that guy you thought was, like, mysterious? If I can just, if you can just let me be that guy again for ten minutes, I know, I know, okay, Tammy, that I can get us from there to being a family. I friggin' know it.

TAMMY looks at him a moment, and then she goes.

Which was of course a lie. But at this point, I'll tell her anything. It's funny, being the husband in a family, being the man, you're like, it's like it's your fucking job to lie. "I understand." "I can help." "Leave it to me, I'll fix everything." Which is, okay, that's the job, okay. I get that's the job and so now all I want is to try to get better at doing the job.

And so, in my job as the husband, one day, I go back to the new doctor to talk about Tam all over again, and third time to a doctor on this problem, third time totally new info. Now she says: postpartum only goes on for so long. Maybe it's not the baby and hormones making her this way, maybe, at this point, it's her life. And I'm like: "Isn't her life like basically just me at this point?" And then I'm like: "Oh, hang on."

So.

But, like, that's not an excuse, okay? I'm not making an excuse.

Because, one night, Tam and George are out, I don't even begin to guess where or what for, and so, one night, during *America's Next Top Model*, Lisa and I do it. *(points to a spot on the floor)* Right there.

A beat.

(pointing at the couch) And also there.

I'm like, what the fuck, my life's a Japanese cartoon at this point anyway. Everything fucking hurts and nothing makes sense. So

I go: what the fuck. And for the first time in my whole life, my philosophy of what the fuck totally lets me down.

What happened was, let me paint you the picture, we were doing it for the second time, here, like I said, and the baby starts wailing, and so I go get her, and I'm trying to change her, and Lisa is like, being her relentless self, and so when Tam and George come home, we're all there, and we're all naked on the couch. All three of us.

And George. Can I just say, George was great through all of it. Really understanding, and, like, gentle, and, like, he's just, like, a helluva guy. George is a helluva guy. And I'm standing here, and George is standing there. And you're Tammy, looking at douchebag me over here and the truly understanding and sensitive George over there.

> *TAMMY and GEORGE enter from another room in the apartment. GEORGE has suitcases and TAMMY has the baby in the stroller. A pause; they're in a kind of confused standoff.*

GEORGE   I will come back this afternoon, to dismantle the crib.

> *A beat.*

I would prefer it, Todd, if you were not here.

TODD   No shit.

> *A pause.*

TAMMY   Okay.

> *TODD shifts, allowing them to get to the apartment door. GEORGE has his hands full and struggles with the knob. TODD watches but does not help. During this suspended moment the baby squalls and then is quiet. GEORGE manages the knob and they go.*

TODD   So, then that happened.

Which isn't stellar narration, I know, but.

And I'm mad, right? Like, this is where waiting got me. This is what being an adult got me. This is what what the fuck got me.

> *The sound of a key in the lock and then* GEORGE *enters. He has a couple of screwdrivers. He looks around then exits to the bedroom.* TODD *watches him.*

I wasn't here for this part.

And I'm like: fuck them. I'm mad, here, in this apartment—I get the apartment, to myself, but it's not like I can be thrilled at that development, you know? Alone where it happened. It's not... it doesn't exactly hum with good memories. Pete calls, he knows all about it, he's all sorry. Like: fuck him, he probably helped them do it, or maybe he gave them the idea, but for sure, at least, he and God and their friends knew about this before I did.

> GEORGE *re-enters with the crib mattress, placing it by the door. He returns to the bedroom.*

How did that happen? Is the thing I ask, to nobody, here. Here. Like, wandering, crazy mad, here's where the baby slept, here's where she ate, here's where she pooed that time with no diaper on, here's this, here's that, and, like, I'm pissed off. I am pissed off. I hope I'm making that absolutely clear with my narration.

> GEORGE *re-enters with pieces of the crib, which he places by the door. He leaves a screwdriver by the door.*

And, like, let me ask you this: do you know what you smell like? Do you have any idea what you walk around smelling like? And, like, the answer to that question is no. You don't. You have no idea what you smell like. People smell other people, not themselves.

During the following GEORGE *re-enters with a side of the crib. There's a mobile attached to it. He finds the screwdriver and attempts to detach the mobile.* TODD *watches him while he speaks to us.*

But, so, like, here I am, bouncing off the walls here. Mad like I've never been mad before. And just when I think I've got a handle on my madness, on the size of it, I stop where I'm walking, and I smell myself. Like, I'm coming out of the bedroom, about to go into the little room we were using for the baby, no reason, I'm just wandering around here, right, because I'm mad, and, like, my own smell, sort of wafts past me because I stop in my tracks.

Which just makes me, like... *now* I'm mad. The smell of myself, the surprise of it, just about made me crazy. I don't know why. Maybe because this place, it used to smell like everybody *except* me. Which is when I did what George asked, and walked out of the apartment.

GEORGE *is struggling with the mobile.* TODD *loses his train as he watches.*

No, you have to, there's a little bit there you have to pop off and the screw is underneath it. You...

(to us) I want, I want to talk more about this. Because, I don't know, you're here, I'm here, what the fuck. If I can't at least make you see the completeness of my madness, then I'm a shit narrator. And you're out like forty bucks. So.

GEORGE *struggles.*

No, you have to— It's. No.

(to us) Like: there's Tammy. And I'm like... Uuuugh. You know? Like, did she, did she give up without telling me? And I wonder what I could have done to help her, right? All the things I ever got told, were, like, just...

(He's watching GEORGE.*)* ...just, like, wait it out and— Fuck. I'm *glad* I wasn't here to watch this.

(to GEORGE*)* No, a different friggin' screwdriver isn't gonna help. You got to—

(to us) The point is, we made an agreement, right? Me and Tam? That's what it is, an agreement. But the thing about an agreement is—

(to GEORGE*)* Fuck, dude, you're killing me. Here.

> *He grabs the mobile and the screwdriver. He works silently for a few beats as* GEORGE *watches.*

The thing about an agreement is, it's only an agreement as long as everyone agrees. Getting married? It's not a locked thing. It doesn't bind anything. It's only an agreement as long as everyone constantly says yes. Over and over. All day long. "Are we married?" "Yes." "Are we married?" "Yes." "Are we still married?" "Yes we are."

GEORGE   That is this country.

TODD   What do you mean?

GEORGE   This place. It is a construction of yes. You make an idea into a real place by saying yes, over and over.

TODD   But, what if I don't feel like saying yes?

GEORGE   Well. Then you wait.

> *A beat.*

TODD   Yeah. Okay.

> TODD *hands the now separated pieces to* GEORGE.

(to us) Like, that would have been an awesome conversation. But I wasn't here for that part. I WAS here for this part:

> *TODD leaves and immediately unlocks the door and opens it. A pause between the two men.*

(of the mobile in GEORGE's hand) I see you got the...

> *A pause.*

GEORGE Todd—

TODD George, I, fuck. I—

GEORGE Todd. I—

TODD What, George? What.

> *A pause.*

GEORGE Todd. I have earned my gifts. All of them.

TODD But.

GEORGE All of them.

> *A beat.*

TODD Fuck you, George.

GEORGE *(sadly)* Yes.

> *TODD walks downstage and GEORGE disappears.*

TODD Fuck him. Fuck George Ambali. Am I right?

> *A beat.*

Am I happy. What do I do.

A pause.

Now, look. I don't want to tell you how to live your life. Although, technically, as the narrator, I pretty much can.

There's a shitload of stuff here that we get for free. And we don't even notice it. Free shit. Water. Shit like that. Cars can drive, women can vote. Every so often, there's a park. Some drunk can get his shit together and make soda pop.

So, like, what's the cost of that? Of all that free shit? Not taxes, shut up already and pay your taxes. I'm saying, what is the cost of that?

Well, basically, the cost of having a place that a guy would walk all the way from Ethiopia to get here is, people are going to walk all the way from Ethiopia to get here. And when they do, they're allowed to take some of your free shit.

And, so there's me, now it feels like I've got nothing, and in a corner, and there's George, who walked here because someone said he could, and the feeling is: "Fuck you, George." Which is, okay, you're gonna have that feeling, I don't care who you are. *That's* human nature. So the question is, you're all, "Fuck you George," but what do you do next? You've got that feeling, you're personally fucked, you've got nothing, and so what are you gonna do, mister, there in your apartment that smells like you exclusively? And, like, I don't want to tell you what to do, but I think what you do is:

> *The following is projected over* TODD's *head. He turns to read it.*

> Suck it the fuck up and apply some courage. Testicle up, big guy.
> —Todd Going

Am I right?

Which is a hard thing? Not hard like trying to avoid a guy with a machete, not hard like standing there watching your kids starve, but still, hard.

Saying "Fuck George" brings you into the territory of, like, fairness, which makes things worse, like I said. It's easy, and it's fun to do, and you feel briefly better when you do it, FUCK GEORGE, and it just makes things worse. The hard thing makes you better.

Not feel better. Let's be clear. You still feel mostly like shit. But, like, since when is everything about whether or not I'm happy? It's possible there's actually more important shit than whether or not some guy feels happy.

LISA, quite pregnant, comes in, hands him a screwdriver.

LISA   Oh, fuck off. You're happy. He's happy. Don't worry about him.

TODD   What are you doing? Don't narrate to them.

LISA   Hey, dickwad. I'll narrate whatever I like to whoever I like. Get to work.

TODD   You want me to what?

LISA   Get to work.

TODD   Get to what?

LISA   Get to work.

TODD   You sure?

LISA   Get to work!

TODD   Oh. Okay.

> *They kiss.* TODD *goes to the pile of crib makings, begins to construct.*

LISA   Dinner's almost ready.

TODD   Right on.

> *She goes.*

I mean, they live just downstairs, anyway. I get the baby pretty much whenever I want. And the guy's still my boss. So.

What the fuck.

> *He works, the lights begin to fade.*

So, like, to review: adulthood. Mostly shameful, confusing, and painful. Doctors fuckin' blow, and the boat show is an awesome place to take your first wife. Women are ridiculously easy to get pregnant, and people will—

LISA   *(from off)* Hey! Look what I stole from work!

> *She enters with a huge framed photograph, a sunflower that's been photoshopped so that it's magenta, on a scorching blue background. It was undeniably present during the coffee shop scene in act one.*

TODD   You stole that?

LISA   I walked right out with it. Nobody said anything. Took it right off the wall.

TODD   Fucking *why.*

LISA   I always liked it.

TODD   What, for, like, here?

LISA   Yeah.

TODD   But it's pretty fucking ugly.

LISA   I like it. I'm putting it up.

TODD   But...

LISA   What? It's our apartment.

TODD   I was here first, though. That's not fair.

LISA   That's not *what*, ballsack? I'm sorry?

TODD   Uh. Okay. Never mind.

(to us) The end.

Blackout.

Michael Healey performed in his first one-act play in 1996 as part of the Fringe Festival of Toronto. Since then, he has become an exceptional voice in Canadian theatre. With an outstanding breadth of work, Healey has won a number of awards as a playwright, including five Dora Mavor Moore Awards, a Governor General's Literary Award, and a Chalmers Playwriting Award. Healey is currently a playwright-in-residence at Tarragon Theatre.